"Should be a first port of call for American voters sadly misinformed about their federal budget. . . . Wessel's aim is to explain for a general audience the basics of the budget–where the money comes from and goes to–and to make the explanation interesting. He succeeds."

—*Financial Times*

"This is the most useful book on government spending since the publication of the classic work, *The Debt and the Deficit* by Robert Heilbroner and Peter Bernstein. In the service of economic literacy, I wish that a few members of the House and the Senate would read the entire book aloud on the floor of the respective chambers (but don't hold your breath)."

—*Huffington Post*

"The federal budget is an inherently complex subject that could easily become boring. But Wessel staves off yawns by painting miniature portraits of lovable wonks from across the spectrum. . . . He gets right to the core of the problem: big-ticket programs that much of the public loves but few want to pay for."

—*Reason*

"An extraordinarily useful book . . . for people unfamiliar with the ins and outs of the federal budget, it should be required reading. For those who already know their way around government finances, it is still a handy resource, but at the same time deeply depressing."

—*Salon.com*

"[Wessel] is blessed with the ability to make the obscure and arcane comprehensible."

—*Canada Free Press*

"Packed with facts and figures–not normally the sort of material that makes for riveting story-telling. Yet the plot of Red Ink is fascinating and frightening."

—*Daytona Beach News-Journal*

"When laid out in front of us in the calm and talented hand of Wessel, we begin to understand in more detail exactly what we're deciding on, and that while it's not going to be easy, fixing the deficit is entirely doable. . . . If you're interested in that dialogue and in further education instead of sound bites and the pontification of pundits this election season, then this is certainly a book for you."

—*800 CEO Read*

"A highly informative volume designed to give voters a grip on what exactly is at stake. . . . Wessel doesn't tell you how to think, but he does give you the facts to think more clearly about what needs to be done."

—*Kirkus Reviews*

"The inner workings of the federal budget and where the money goes by economics expert David Wessel. . . . Controversy over whether tax increases of spending cuts should be made to defense, Medicare, or Social Security spending provides fuel for great debate."

—*Booklist*

"A timely analysis."

—*Library Journal*

"*Red Ink* is the most concise, understandable, and focused book I have read about the dire problems we now face because of our burgeoning deficits and debt. It is not a pretty tale, but it is a tale all informed citizens should know."

—David M. Rubenstein, co-chief executive officer, The Carlyle Group

"Stop. Buy this book, or at least read the first chapter. David Wessel explains the approaching debt crisis in clear, concise, nonpartisan plain English. It will not only scare your pants off, it will motivate you to call your congressman and scream, 'For God's sake, enough partisanship, save America, cut spending, raise revenue, whatever! But do it and do it now.'"

—Erskine Bowles, former chief of staff for Bill Clinton and co-chairman of Barack Obama's National Commission on Fiscal Responsibility

"In *Red Ink* David Wessel has accomplished two miracles: he has made a budget book interesting and he has deciphered the behavior of Washington for Americans beyond the Beltway. Nicely done."

—Douglas Holtz-Eakin, former director of the Congressional Budget Office

"David Wessel's *Red Ink* is a wise and pithy introduction to the great economic issue of our time."

—N. Gregory Mankiw, professor of Economics, Harvard University

"I wish every voter would read this book. It spells out in a clear, non-partisan way the realities of the deficit, how we got here, and the hard choices that lie ahead. The message is painful, but the book is not–it is engaging, thoughtful, and a pleasure to read."

—Christina D. Romer, former Chair of the Council of Economic Advisers and current professor of Economics at the University of California, Berkeley

"David Wessel does a first rate job at providing insight into complex fiscal issues. Anyone wanting to understand key players, pivotal moments, and high stakes in the critical issue of America's long-term unsustainable debts would be very well served by *Red Ink*."

—Peter G. Peterson, former U.S. Secretary of Commerce, founder of the Peter G. Peterson Foundation, and author of the bestseller, *Running on Empty*

RED
INK

ALSO BY DAVID WESSEL

In Fed We Trust

Prosperity (with Bob Davis)

RED

Inside the High-Stakes Politics
of the Federal Budget

INK

David Wessel

CROWN
BUSINESS

NEW YORK

Published in the United States by Crown Business, an imprint of the
Crown Publishing Group, a division of Random House, Inc., New York.

www.crownpublishing.com

CROWN BUSINESS is a trademark and CROWN and the Rising Sun colophon
are registered trademarks of Random House, Inc.

Originally published in hardcover in the United States
by Crown Business, an Imprint of the Crown Publishing Group,
a division of Random House, Inc., New York, in 2012.

Library of Congress Cataloging-in-Publication Data
Wessel, David.
Red ink: inside the high-stakes politics of the federal budget / David Wessel.
    p.   cm.
Includes bibliographical references and index.
1. Budget–United States.   2. Budget deficits–United States.   3. Deficit
financing–United States.   4. Debts, Public–United States.   I. Title.
HJ2051.W427 2012
336.73–dc23   2012011819

ISBN 978-0-7704-3616-2
eISBN 978-0-7704-3615-5

Book design by Ellen Cipriano
Illustrations by Nelson Hsu
Cover design by Laura Duffy
Cover photographs: Getty Images:
(corn) Burazin; (jet) Tim Ridley; (flag) C Squared Studios;
(stethoscope) Jules Frazier; (cart) James Worrell;
(food stamps) Brand X Pictures; (Capitol) Imagemore Co., Ltd.;
(prescription bottle) Don Farrall; (ship) Stocktrek Images

First Paperback Edition

146122990

FOR JULIA AND BEN

CONTENTS

CHAPTER I

SPENDING $400 MILLION AN HOUR

In the cold predawn darkness of Monday, February 13, 2012, Robert Friedlander walked into a Starbucks three blocks from the White House. As they had been instructed by e-mail the night before, a half dozen reporters were waiting for him—one each from Dow Jones, Bloomberg, Reuters, Associated Press, Politico, and the *Washington Post*. With no ceremony and not much conversation, the young White House budget office aide slipped each of them a CD in a plain, square white envelope. The contents: President Barack Obama's budget for the coming fiscal year. "It's embargoed until 11:15," he said. Friedlander's inside-the-Beltway shorthand meant the reporters had about five hours to scour the documents before publishing stories on newswires and websites. At 11:15 A.M., the president was to begin speaking about the budget at a northern Virginia community college.

Every president since Warren Harding has been required by law to send an annual budget to Congress. It's the only time that the chief executive of the United States has to make his promises add up. The modern version comes in three formats: free online, $27 for the CD, or $218 for the printed four-volume paperback set. The budget is one part rhetoric by the party in power that highlights—depending on the times—the government's largesse or its tightfistedness. A second part details how the president would, if Congress went along, spend a sum equal to the value of all the goods and services produced by the 82 million people of Germany, the world's fifth-largest economy. And in its modern form, a third part is dire prediction, a collection of uncomfortable, indisputable facts showing the unsustainable fiscal course the U.S. government is on.

The budget doesn't record what might have been. The document Obama released in February did not, for instance, acknowledge intense summertime talks the president had with Republican House Speaker John Boehner that failed to end a stalemate over spending and taxes. And for all its excruciating detail, the president's budget doesn't ultimately settle anything; the Constitution gives Congress the power to tax and spend. But neither is "presbud"—as it's known to insiders on the congressional committees that decide how to spend taxpayers' money—irrelevant. The budget is the starting point for an annual round of maneuvering that ranges from high-minded debate about national priorities and "hard choices" to big-money lobbying and small favors for home-state constituents. The details buried in it—which programs should live and which should die, which should get more and which should get less—often become law.

Ultimately, the federal government's power comes in three

forms: its physical force, both foreign and domestic; its ability to make and enforce rules that govern our lives; and its power to tax and spend. The budget—and this book—is about the third form. With far more precision than thirty-second sound bites or campaign stump speeches, the president's budget and alternatives crafted by the opposition in Congress reflect contrasting visions for the size of government in America and the role it plays in the economy. How strong and generous a safety net should government provide to the poor? How much should taxpayers invest in medical research? How hard should government lean against market forces that are widening the gap between winners and losers in the economy? How much should spending be cut to rein in the deficit, and how much should taxes be raised, if at all?

Anyone in Washington who is serious about trying to steer the government to the right or to the left understands the power and import of decisions on taxes and spending embodied in the budget. Among them are Jack Lew and Paul Ryan, both steeped in fiscal details big and small. The two illustrate the competing visions for government and the use of the budget as an important, perhaps the only important, way to achieve them. As director of the White House Office of Management and Budget, Lew, fifty-six, put the finishing touches on Obama's February plan just as the president named him White House chief of staff. Ryan, forty-two, a Republican congressman from Wisconsin and the chairman of the House Budget Committee, promptly criticized the Obama budget–"broken promises, failed leadership and a diminished future," he said–and set to work on an alternative.

Jacob "Jack" Lew got his start in politics in 1968, at age twelve, as a volunteer for anti–Vietnam War presidential candidate Eugene McCarthy. Lew has never run for office, but he has been at the elbow of influential Democrats from the late House Speaker Tip O'Neill and New York congresswoman Bella Abzug to Secretary of State Hillary Clinton and President Obama. An Orthodox Jew who avoids working on Friday nights and Saturdays except when duty calls, Lew is truly convinced of the government's power to do good. When he took over the budget office, he replaced the portrait of Alexander Hamilton that had been hung by his predecessor, Peter Orszag, with paintings of his native New York City done by artists working for the government's Works Progress Administration in the 1930s.

Lew is tall and lanky, his thick black hair just beginning to gray and his oval wire-rim glasses exactly what one would expect of a budget wonk. But Lew, who also was budget director for Bill Clinton, is the sort of wonk who can say sincerely: "I have a soft spot for Medicaid"–the government health insurance program for the poor funded jointly by state and federal governments–"because it's the thing that's easy for the political system to mischaracterize.

"For the most part, it's a lot of people who don't have insurance, who are poor. Slashing it would mean we'd be in a world where the most vulnerable were getting sicker and sicker and ultimately showing up in the hospital."

Jack Lew believes in government. The budget is a means to that end. "The purpose of power is to get things done," he once said. "Budgets aren't books of numbers. They're a tapestry, the fabric of what we believe. The numbers tell a story, a self-portrait of what we are as a country."

Paul Ryan is wiry, intense, energetic, and just as sincere as Lew—in the opposite direction. His quest: to limit the size of government, including spending less on Medicaid and almost everything else. His weapon of choice: the budget. In 2007, he vaulted over more senior congressmen to become the ranking Republican on the House Budget Committee, which is charged with crafting an annual budget blueprint for Congress. He became chairman in 2011 when Republicans took control of the House.

Like Jack Lew, Ryan came to politics young, as a college intern with the foreign policy adviser to Senator Robert Kasten from his home state of Wisconsin. Later he worked for a think tank organized by influential conservative Republicans Jack Kemp and Bill Bennett and for Sam Brownback, then a Republican senator from Kansas. Eleven days after turning twenty-eight, Ryan announced he was running for Congress from southeastern Wisconsin—and ended up with 57.2 percent of the vote in 1998, a stunning margin in a district that, as Ryan notes frequently, went for Democrats Bill Clinton, Al

Gore, and Barack Obama. He has won even bigger majorities ever since.

With the conviction and clarity that have conservatives salivating over him as a future presidential candidate, Ryan says, "I do believe government has a role in making sure we have a safety net to help people who cannot help themselves or are temporarily down on their luck, but I don't want to see government turn that safety net into a hammock."

Unlike Jack Lew, Paul Ryan doesn't wear glasses. He had Lasik surgery in 2000. The surgery isn't generally covered by insurance; the patient pays cash. Ryan has built that into his stump speech on why free markets can cure the health care cost of disease. "It cost me $2,000 an eye. Since then, it's been revolutionized three times and now costs $800 an eye," he says. "This sector isn't immune from free-market principles."

Ryan stands out among conservative Republicans in Congress: he puts numbers behind his vision of a smaller government, proposing to spend less on almost everything and turn federal health and other benefit programs into vouchers. "We've defined ourselves by putting our cards on the table with our budget. And we added more specificity than most budgets have had in the past because I think the time demands it and the numbers require it," he says. That's made him as big a target for the left as he is a hero to the right. One liberal group in 2011 ran an ad showing him pushing an old lady in a wheelchair off a cliff. Ryan has had personal experience with the safety net. At age sixteen, he collected Social Security survivor benefits after his dad died. Critics charge that makes him a hypocrite for pushing to scale back Social Security. He answers that, without change, the program is headed for certain collapse.

Off and on for the past thirty years, the federal budget and the budget deficit–the difference between what the government takes in and what it spends–have pushed their way onto newspaper front pages and widely read blogs, into presidential debates and congressional hearings, into AARP ads and Business Roundtable press releases, into calculations of traders on Wall Street and strategies of the secretive managers of China's foreign-exchange hoard, estimated at a staggering $3 trillion. Occasionally, talk about spending and taxes and deficits and debt even pops up in the kitchen-table and bar-stool conversations of ordinary Americans–the ones who pay the taxes, count on Social Security and Medicare, and elect the members of Congress who have, so far, been unable to fix what ails the national government's finances.

The Washington jargon of budgeteers like Lew and Ryan excludes rather than informs the citizenry. It is peppered with words like *baseline, authorization, appropriation, entitlement,* and *expenditure,* and phrases like "Byrd droppings" and "changes in mandatory program spending," or CHIMPS. The scale of the budget is overwhelming, the numbers so huge they are impossible to comprehend. As humor columnist Dave Barry once wrote, the dimensions of the federal budget are hard to grasp because millions, billions, and trillions sound so much alike.

One has to think about golf balls, watermelons, and hot-air balloons to get an idea of the magnitudes.

In fiscal year 2011–from October 1, 2010, to September 30, 2011–the federal government spent $3.6 *trillion,* $400 million an hour, more than $30,000 per American household. By any measure, that's a lot of money. In chapter 3, I'll look more closely at where the money goes. But for now, a few observations:

Nearly two-thirds of annual federal spending is on autopilot and doesn't require an annual vote by Congress.

Congress does have to pass legislation every year to keep the government operating. When it delays until the federal fiscal year begins on October 1, as it has lately, scares percolate about a government shutdown in which workers deemed "nonessential" would be told to stay home, national parks would be closed, and bureaucrats' phones would go unanswered. But much of the money the government spends–nearly 63 percent in 2011–goes out the door every year without any affirmative vote of Congress. Social Security benefits get deposited. Health care bills for Medicare for the elderly and disabled and Medicaid for the poor are paid. Food stamps are issued. Farm subsidy checks are written. Interest payments are dutifully made to holders of Treasury bonds. Congress can alter these programs, but if it does nothing, the money is spent. As Eugene Steuerle, a Treasury economist in the Reagan years who is now at the Urban Institute think tank in Washington, puts it: "In 2009, for the first time in the nation's history, every dollar of revenues had been committed before Congress walked in the door." The government's total take was only enough to pay for promises that had been made in the past–interest, Social Security, Medicare, Medicaid, and so on. For everything else, the government had to borrow.

The U.S. defense budget is greater than the *combined* defense budgets of the next seventeen largest spenders.

The United States spends about $700 billion a year on its military. That's more than the combined military budgets of China, the United Kingdom, France, Russia, Japan, Saudi Arabia, Germany, India, Italy, Brazil, South Korea, Australia, Canada, Turkey, the United Arab Emirates, Spain, and Israel. Generals and admirals counter that the United States asks its military to do more than the forces of all those countries combined as well–to keep sea lanes open for international trade, for instance, and to be prepared to deploy almost anywhere. In all, $1 of every $5 the federal government spent in 2011 went to defense, and about 20 cents of that $1 was spent on the wars in Iraq and Afghanistan.

For every dollar the United States spends on the military,

it spends another nickel on foreign aid, international development aid, and humanitarian assistance. Yet in a CNN poll in March 2011, the typical respondent estimated about 10 percent of the entire federal budget goes for "aid to foreign countries for international development and humanitarian assistance." The reality: about 1 percent. That's another problem with budgeting: the public makes woefully wrong assumptions about virtually every aspect of it.

Firing every federal government employee wouldn't save enough to even cut the deficit in half.

Wages and benefits for everyone from the president to air force pilots to postal service clerks cost $435 billion in 2011. In all, the federal government employs 4.4 million workers, measured as full-time equivalents. About 35 percent are uniformed military personnel and another 29 percent are civilians working for the departments of Defense, Veterans Affairs, and Homeland Security. Wages and benefits account for $1 of every $8 the government spends, not an insignificant sum. But eliminating the federal workforce entirely would have pared the federal budget deficit in 2011 by only one-third.

Where does the rest of the money go? A lot of what government does is siphon money from some and give it to others, or occasionally to the same people. About $2.3 trillion, two-thirds of all federal spending last year, went to benefits of some sort for individuals: Social Security, Medicare, Medicaid, food stamps. Another $220 billion went for grants to state and local governments for everything from schools in poor neighborhoods to sewage-treatment plants.

"It's the things that people want that are causing the problem," Jack Lew says. "People have this feeling that others are getting the benefit, but when you look at what's driving the deficit, it's Social Security that people very much want. It's Medicare that people very much want. It's Medicaid, which is the long-term care program that means that people don't have their eighty-year-old mothers and fathers living in the guest room when they need round-the-clock care."

About $1 of every $4 the federal government spends goes to health care today, and that share is rising inexorably.

For all the talk about avoiding a government-run health care system in the United States, about half of all spending on health already comes from federal, state, and local governments. The heart of federal health care spending is Medicare and Medicaid. In 1981, they accounted for 9.5 percent of all federal outlays besides interest. By 2011, the two programs were consuming nearly 25 percent of all outlays, the result of three decades in which health care costs have risen more rapidly than almost anything else and the number of people reliant on the government programs has grown. In 2021, if current policies remain in place, government spending on health care will consume 33 percent of federal spending, according to the Congressional Budget Office (CBO), the nonpartisan arm of Congress that tracks such things. The Medicare prescription drug benefit alone will cost the government more over time than the wars in Afghanistan and Iraq. The spending on the wars will end someday; the drug benefit is permanent.

Nearly all the growth in the federal budget over the next ten years is going to come from spending on health care and interest payments unless something changes. "You can't fix this without doing health care," says Paul Ryan. "I mean, health care is the driver of our debt." And, as he and others routinely observe, even though the United States spends far more per person on health care than any other country, it isn't close to having the world's healthiest population.

The $700 billion bank bailout didn't cost taxpayers nearly as much as initially feared.

The financial crisis was an economic calamity. It provoked the worst recession since the Great Depression, the cost of which went far beyond the boundaries of the federal budget. The Great Recession, as it became known, wiped out $7 trillion in home equity. Two and a half years after the economy had resumed growing, nearly 13 million Americans were still out of work. The United States faced significant deficits even before the recession, but the size of today's record-busting budget deficits are, in large measure, the consequence of revenues lost, taxes cut, and spending increased because of the recession.

In rescuing the banks, the big insurance company American International Group (AIG), money market mutual funds, and automakers General Motors and Chrysler, the government–that is, the taxpayers–took enormous risks. "At one point, the federal government guaranteed or insured $4.4 trillion in face value of financial assets. If the financial system had suffered another shock on the road to recovery, taxpayers would have faced staggering losses," the bailout's Congressional Oversight Panel concluded in its final report. Indeed, private investors who risked their money to shore up big financial institutions–Warren Buffett, for one–demanded much better returns than the government did.

But actual direct cost to taxpayers for the much-maligned bailout of the banks proved to be a lot lower than expected. The sticker price on the Troubled Asset Relief Program (TARP) was $700 billion, the mind-blowing sum that George W. Bush and his Treasury secretary, Hank Paulson, got from Congress in October 2008. As of the end of March 2012, the Treasury said it had disbursed or promised only $470 billion of the $700 billion. In the end, it turned out, the banks didn't need all the money that Congress authorized, and the government didn't spend all $50 billion Congress originally earmarked for beleaguered homeowners.

By early 2012, about 67 percent of the money that went out had been paid back with interest, another $12 billion had been written off, and much of the remainder looked likely to be recouped. The biggest losses to taxpayers are expected to come not from the banks but from AIG and GM; the ultimate cost depends on the price of the AIG and GM shares the government holds. At last tally, the CBO and the White House Office of Management and Budget projected the ultimate cost of the program will be between $32 billion (CBO) and $60 billion (OMB). But the headline is the same: the cost is significantly less than the hundreds of billions the agencies–and the media–anticipated in the darkest days of the financial crisis.

The biggest direct hit to taxpayers from the financial crisis, so far, isn't from TARP, but from the bailouts of Fannie Mae and Freddie Mac, the mortgage giants that were created by the government, later turned into private companies, and effectively nationalized in 2008. As of December 2011, the government had pumped a net of $151 billion into them and they weren't close to standing on their own. The ultimate cost depends on housing prices.

The share of income most American families pay in federal taxes has been falling for more than thirty years. Today, Americans pay less of their income in taxes than citizens of nearly every other developed country.

There are a dozen ways to measure the slice of income that the government takes in taxes, and most point in the same direction. One meaningful metric: the CBO estimates that for families in the very middle of the middle class, the federal government took an average of 19.2 percent of their gross (before deductions) income in 1981 in income, payroll, and all other federal taxes. State and local taxes have risen for some since then, but the federal tax bite has eased. In 2007, just before the recession hit, according to the CBO, the tax take for these Americans was 14.3 percent—and it has fallen since. The Tax Policy Center, a joint venture of two Washington think tanks, the Urban Institute and the Brookings Institution, estimates that the folks in the middle of the middle paid 12.4 percent of their income in taxes in 2011.

Nearly half of American households—46 percent—didn't pay any federal *income* taxes at all in 2011. It's not that they all cheated, though some did. Rather, the vast majority didn't make enough money to owe taxes, or they took advantage of tax breaks that Congress has created to help the working poor, the elderly, and students, or to reward investors who put money into municipal bonds or other favored investments. About half of those who didn't owe federal *income* taxes were hit by *payroll* taxes levied on wages to finance Social Security and Medicare.

Americans turn over less of their income to local, state, and federal governments than citizens of almost any other rich country, even when taking into account that budgets of foreign governments often include the cost of providing health care for all, and in the United States less than a third of the populace gets health insurance through the government. The Organization for Economic Cooperation and Development, a Paris-based consortium of developed-country governments that makes apples-to-apples comparisons, says government at all levels in the United States took in taxes about 25 percent of the income in the economy in 2010. Twenty-seven countries took more, including Japan (27 percent), Canada (31 percent), the United Kingdom (35 percent), Germany (36 percent), and France (43 percent).

The federal government gives up almost as much money from tax loopholes, deductions, credits, and all other tax breaks as it collects in individual and corporate income tax.

The U.S. tax code is like a big piece of Swiss cheese. It has a lot of holes. Over time, Congress and presidents have cut new holes and expanded old ones. Taxpayers and their clever lawyers and accountants have also enlarged the holes, sometimes with help from the courts. More holes means the government has to get more money from somewhere else. All these tax breaks added up to about $1.1 trillion in 2011. That is approaching the total take of $1.3 trillion from the individual and corporate income tax.

When "tax cuts" are politically popular and "government spending" is not, politicians favor new or bigger tax breaks over spending increases–to help college kids meet tuition bills, to encourage energy companies to develop alternatives to fossil fuels, you name it. This "spending through the tax code," as it is sometimes called, is cherished by those who benefit and pushes up tax rates needed to finance the government. Hence, the growing enthusiasm for "tax reform" that would eliminate some of these tax breaks and bring down tax rates. But–and there's always a *but* in these conversations–the bigger income tax breaks are by far the most popular: allowing homeowners to deduct mortgage interest payments and excluding employer-paid health insurance premiums from workers' taxable income.

For every dollar the U.S. government spent in 2011, it borrowed 36 cents, much of it from China, where the income per person is about one-sixth of that in the United States.

Except for four unusual years at the end of the 1990s and the beginning of the 2000s, the federal government has spent more than it took in every year for the past four decades. It borrows the difference, essentially promising that taxpayers in the future will pick up the tab for government spending today. The U.S. government is by far the world's biggest borrower even though the United States is by far the world's biggest and richest economy, a historical anomaly. By any yardstick, its borrowing in recent years has been huge. Part of this was automatic: when people are out of work, they pay less in taxes, and government spending on unemployment benefits and food stamps goes up because more people qualify. Part of this was deliberate policy: Congress increased spending and cut taxes.

The bottom line is that the U.S. government borrowed $3.6 billion a day in 2011, holidays and weekends included, or about $11,500 for every man, woman, and child in the country. About half of that borrowing *came from overseas.* The net interest tab on the government debt was about $230 billion last year, which exceeded the budgets of the departments of Commerce, Education, Energy, Homeland Security, Interior, Justice, and State, plus the federal courts, *combined.* As deficits persist and interest rates rise from recent very low levels, as they inevitably will, interest payments will claim an increasing slice of the federal budget, crowding out spending on other things.

Today's budget deficit is not an economic problem— tomorrow's is.

For all the dire rhetoric about the dangers of debt, all the scares about the United States becoming another (albeit far larger) Greece, big U.S. government deficits have not been an economic problem—at least not yet.

The deficits have been big. Measured against the value of all the goods and services produced in the United States, known as the gross domestic product (GDP), deficits in the

Ronald Reagan years peaked at 6 percent. In the past three years, they came in at 10 percent of GDP in 2009 (the fiscal year that spans the end of the George W. Bush presidency and the beginning of Barack Obama's) and at 9 percent and 8.7 percent in the two subsequent years.

Running bigger deficits in a deep recession and sluggish recovery is still Economics 101—even if one can get a good debate going among serious people about how best to do that and how well the medicine works. Running *deficits* means the government has to borrow the difference between income and outgo. The sum of all that borrowing is the government *debt*. Borrowing by government, banks, business, and consumers soared so much during the 2000s that at the end of 2008 the U.S. economy as a whole owed twice as much as it did in 1975, measured against the size of the economy. Since then, private borrowing has come down, but government borrowing has gone up—a lot—in a deliberate effort to cushion the economy from the pain caused when so many lenders pull back and so many borrowers try to pay off loans or walk away from them.

Despite the anxiety about the capacity of a paralyzed political system to grapple with deficits projected for the future—and despite the headline-making move by ratings agency Standard & Poor's to strip the U.S. Treasury of the prized AAA credit rating that signifies the safest risks—savers, investors, and governments around the world still view U.S. Treasury bonds as the most secure place to put their money. For now. The only other big government bond markets—Europe and Japan—are in places that have big problems of their own, which makes the United States the world's tallest midget. What's more, the flood of money from all over the world has pushed down the interest rate that the U.S. Treasury pays to fifty-year lows. But this ability to borrow enormous sums at incredibly low interest rates cannot and will not last forever, even if no one can say exactly when the day of reckoning will arrive.

"A lot of us . . . didn't see this last crisis as it came upon us. This one is really easy to see," says Erskine Bowles, a former investment banker who was Bill Clinton's chief of staff, later cochairman of an Obama-appointed commission on the deficit, and now an unlikely itinerant preacher on the urgency of dealing with the deficit. "The fiscal path we are on today is simply not sustainable. These deficits that we are incurring on an annual basis are like a cancer, and they are truly going to destroy this country from within unless we have the common sense to do something about it.

"We face the most predictable economic crisis in history."

CHAPTER 2

HOW WE GOT HERE

At seventy-four years old, Leon Panetta is one of the few American politicians who can give a truly emotional speech about the federal deficit. Maybe that's because he is one of a generation of thrifty Americans who elected politicians unwilling to fund many of the benefits they promised. Or maybe it's because he has spent so much of his adult life in the belly of government—from the House of Representatives to the White House to, now, the top job at the Pentagon. "This country cannot continue to run trillion-dollar deficits and expect that we can remain a powerful nation," Panetta has said, meshing a little old-time deficit religion with his current job. "When you run those size deficits...the borrowing we have to do around the world...makes us more dependent on those countries that are purchasing our securities. It deprives the country of the resources we need regardless of your priorities. Worst of all, it raises the most regressive tax of all: the tax on our children who have to ultimately pay the interest on that debt."

In textbooks, the chief governmental actors are the president, along with an amorphous institution called Congress, represented by the familiar profile of the Capitol. In the case of the budget, this simple model holds true–to a point. The president and the top leaders of Congress ultimately do make the big calls. But below decks is a squad of people who spend most of their careers contemplating, framing, influencing, negotiating, measuring, and executing decisions about spending and taxes.

Panetta has been one of them. His life spans three-quarters of a century of evolving American fiscal policy, from Franklin D. Roosevelt to Barack Obama. He was born in June 1938 to Italian immigrants, owners of a small Northern California restaurant called Carmelo's Café. At the time, Roosevelt's New Deal was expanding the federal government dramatically. By the time Panetta came to Washington, in the mid-1960s, Lyndon Johnson's Great Society was expanding it further, promising benefits in old age to then young baby boomers (including two of Panetta's three children). As a Democratic congressman from California in the 1980s, Panetta voted for Ronald Reagan's big 1981 tax cut, though he later condemned it as "a dangerous experiment" and a "riverboat gamble."

A decade later, Panetta was among a handful of congressional leaders who cut a deal in 1990 with President George H. W. Bush to raise taxes and cut spending, a move still controversial twenty years later. He was in Bill Clinton's White House when the government ran its first budget surplus in nearly thirty years.

And after a twelve-year hiatus in California, Panetta returned to Washington in 2009 as Obama's CIA director, among those overseeing the killing of Osama bin Laden. In 2011, he became defense secretary, supervising a $700 billion budget, a sum so large that the Pentagon would be among the world's twenty biggest economies if it were a nation. In 2012, the veteran of decades of deficit wars was warning of irreparable damage to U.S. national security if Congress didn't undo legislation that would cut the defense budget in 2013 and beyond. "I've become very eclectic," he says. A natural politician with an easygoing manner, Panetta has a disarming habit of launching a deep belly laugh at his own jokes. He laughs at this line.

In 1938, Panetta's birth year, federal spending came to 7.7 percent of the gross domestic product, or GDP, the value of all the goods and services produced in the United States that year. That simple ratio–the government spent almost 8 cents for every dollar of goods and services produced in America–prevents us from being confused by the changes that occur over time, such as the effects of inflation or the simple fact that America is not the same place it was three-quarters of a century ago.

In 1938, for example, you could buy a pair of denim overalls out of the Sears catalog for 95 cents; in 2012, the same overalls cost $39.99, roughly forty times more. Adjusted only for inflation, federal spending has increased nearly thirtyfold since 1938. But the United States today has twice as many people as it did in 1938, which increases the cost of government the same

Money In and Money Out, Percentage of Economy

Measured against all the goods and services produced in the United States, the gross domestic product, spending during the Great Recession rose to the highest levels since World War II and its aftermath, while revenues fell.

Percentage of GDP

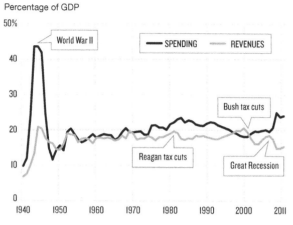

Source: White House Office of Management and Budget

Money In and Money Out, Adjusted for Inflation

Federal spending, adjusted for inflation, has climbed steadily for the past sixty years. Revenues lately haven't climbed, hence big budget deficits.

Billions of 2005 dollars

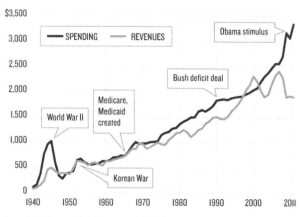

Source: White House Office of Management and Budget

36

way having more kids increases a family's grocery bills. Every week, for example, thirty-two thousand more people enroll in Medicare, the government's health insurance for the elderly.

The United States is also far richer than it was in those Depression years. It can afford more of everything–cars, electronics, massages, restaurant meals, and government. Back then, the entire output of the U.S. economy was about $86 billion at 1938 prices, which is $1.1 trillion in current dollars. Since then the economy has grown to $15.1 trillion. That's a much bigger pie. And the federal government is also spending a far larger share of it, roughly a quarter for every dollar of output, 24.1 percent last year versus 7.7 percent in 1938.

Each decade of the fiscal history of the United States has been the subject of dozens of books. *The Fiscal Revolution in America,* by the late Herbert Stein, an economic adviser to Richard Nixon, ran to over six hundred pages–and that takes the story only through 1994. With budgets, as with so much of life, it's hard to know where you're headed until you know where you've been.

So here's a quick history of the federal budget in six pieces.

THE NEW DEAL: THE BEGINNING OF "BIG GOVERNMENT"

From the end of World War I through the early years of the Great Depression, a "balanced budget" was regarded as an unquestioned virtue, and the U.S. government consistently ran surpluses. Until Congress created a Bureau of the Budget inside the Treasury in 1921, the president didn't even submit an annual budget to Congress. At the end of 1931, Herbert Hoover, committed to the "balance the budget" orthodoxy of the day and determined to maintain the gold standard after the British abandoned it, proposed a tax increase. In words that echo those uttered in the halls of Congress today, Hoover told Congress in December 1931: "The first requirement of confidence and of economic recovery is financial stability of the United States Government. Even with increased taxation, the Government will reach the utmost safe limit of its borrowing capacity." Taxes were raised and the Federal Reserve kept credit too tight. The federal government was smaller–4.3 percent of GDP in 1931–and narrower. About 70 percent of the spending went for three things: defense, veterans' benefits, and interest payments on the national debt. "The federal budget was not then, as it later became, a machine constantly generating new programs and expansions of old ones," Herbert Stein wrote.

The Great Depression was well entrenched when Franklin Delano Roosevelt took office in March 1933. Six days after his inauguration, he picked up the "balanced budget" banner, telling Congress that the federal government was on the road to bankruptcy. "Too often in recent history, liberal governments have been wrecked on the rocks of loose fiscal policy," he said. Roosevelt asked for emergency powers to cut spending and vowed that if they were granted, there was "a reasonable prospect" that within a year, the government's income would be sufficient to cover its spending. He got the power he sought, but the budget wouldn't be balanced until 1947.

Increased government spending was not the centerpiece of FDR's initial program to resuscitate the economy. Indeed, the new president's insistence on personally approving public works projects one by one slowed the flow of money. Instead, FDR sought to thwart a devastating deflation by using government muscle to raise wages and prices, control and plan production and employment, change the price of gold, and expand the supply of credit. "Spending," Stein wrote, "was the ugly duckling of Roosevelt's 1933 barnyard, not to become the swan for several years, and then mainly by default"–that is, after other steps didn't work as hoped or were declared unconstitutional. "Unemployment remained high. Something had to be done, and more spending was left as the only thing that could be done."

Roosevelt's New Deal left an indelible mark on America, some of it physical. The bridges that government-paid workers built back then still punctuate the Merritt Parkway in Connecticut, while Dealey Plaza, scene of John F. Kennedy's assassination, is still a melancholic swath of green in downtown Dallas. Largely because of the growing scale of the federal government, the population of Washington, D.C., grew more in the 1930s–176,000 new residents, a 36 percent increase–

than in the previous two decades combined. Many agencies created then are now permanent fixtures: the Federal Deposit Insurance Corporation, which insures bank deposits; the Federal Housing Administration, which guarantees some mortgages; the Tennessee Valley Authority, which sells electricity; and the Securities and Exchange Commission, which regulates the stock market. In a move with lasting consequences for the power of the presidency, the Bureau of the Budget was moved in 1939 from the Treasury to a new Executive Office of the President, centralizing the preparation of the annual budget in the White House and permanently elevating the president's role in budgeting.

The New Deal left other legacies, too. Tough talk about fiscal rectitude and avoiding debt would persist, but, as Stein wrote in the late 1960s, "Never again would there be a serious effort, like Hoover's of 1932, to balance the budget in a depression or offset the revenue loss caused by the depression itself." In fact, the big economic lesson to take root as a result of the Great Depression, elaborated by Britain's John Maynard Keynes, the twentieth-century economic giant, was that the government and the Federal Reserve had been too stingy and that only government spending pulled the U.S. economy out of the ditch. This view informed the economic strategies of presidents through George W. Bush (who successfully proposed a little-remembered tax cut in 2008 intended to give the economy a lift) and Barack Obama.

Lately, though, Keynesian "truths" have come under attack—in some academic circles first and, more recently, in political circles—as the economy has languished despite massive government efforts to revive it. "In three short years, an unprecedented explosion of spending, with borrowed money, has added trillions to an already unaffordable national debt," Indiana governor Mitch Daniels said in the Republican response to Obama's 2012 State of the Union address. "The President's grand experiment in trickle-down government has held back rather than sped economic recovery. He seems to sincerely believe we can build a middle class out of government jobs paid for with borrowed dollars."

With Social Security—the first of the enduring and popular social programs that enlarged the federal government's role in providing for the poor, sick, and elderly—FDR also planted the seeds of the modern American welfare state and a bigger federal government. When he died in 1945, government spending, swollen by the cost of fighting World War II, exceeded 40 percent of GDP. It fell after the war but would never return to pre-FDR levels.

"From the mid-1930s to the 1970s, the government made a set of commitments that led to expectations on the part of the American people about what their government owes them," says Robert Reischauer, a former director of the Congressional Budget Office. "And they're totally unprepared to go back to a different world."

THE GREAT SOCIETY: GUNS, BUTTER, AND MEDICARE

In the burst of prosperity after World War II, Leon Panetta's parents sold the restaurant and sunk their profits into a twelve-acre walnut farm in Carmel, where Leon and his wife, Sylvia, now live when he's not in Washington. "My dad used to have a pole and hook, and shake every one of these branches, and hit the walnuts," he once said. "And my brother and I used to be underneath collecting the walnuts, putting 'em in sacks. And, you know, my dad often said I was well-trained to go to Washington because I'd been dodging these nuts all my life." Panetta went to college and law school at Santa Clara University, a Jesuit institution, and then did two years in army intelligence.

In 1966, he met the nuts face-to-face.

Rejecting his father's advice to settle down and practice law, he looked instead toward Washington. "I had read about Joe Califano [an aide to LBJ] so I wrote him and said, 'I don't know you. I'm very proud of you as an Italian. I happen to be Italian. Is there a way for me to get involved in government?' Sure enough, he wrote and set up some appointments. . . . I went to the Justice Department. I went to the Pentagon. I went to other agencies, and I decided I wanted to go to Capitol Hill. So I walked into [Senator Tom] Kuchel's office; they had an opening for a legislative assistant. I didn't know the senator, I didn't know anybody there. They looked at my background.

He liked the fact that I was a lawyer, he liked the fact that I had been in the army, and he hired me."

The Congress for which Panetta went to work in 1966 was strikingly different from today's polarized institution in which one party regularly passes major legislation with few votes from the other, and often none. Party lines were far less predictable, in large part because of a cadre of southern Democrats that was considerably more conservative than a sizable group of liberal Republicans, including Kuchel.

Still, Democrats dominated the federal government in 1966. Amid the increasingly unpopular Vietnam War, LBJ was completing the domestic agenda that Roosevelt and his successor, Harry Truman, had laid out. Federal spending rose steadily as Johnson refused to choose, in the lingo of the day, between guns and butter, hitting a peak for that era of 20.5 percent of GDP in 1968. But nothing that Johnson did left a fiscal legacy as enduring as the creation of the all-federal Medicare health insurance program for the aged and Medicaid for the poor, the cost of which is split between state and federal governments. Before Medicare, only about half the elderly had any health insurance. Many employers didn't cover retirees, and much of the available private insurance was lousy. Back then, one in five seniors hadn't seen a doctor in the previous two years; after Medicare, that figure settled at roughly one in twelve. Columbia University economist Frank Lichtenberg estimates that the typical older American spends about 13 percent fewer days sick in bed because of Medicare and that the program has increased the odds that a sixty-five-year-old will make it to age seventy by about 13 percent.

But Medicare is a leading example of the law of unintended consequences. It's a living laboratory. Science moves in unpredictable spurts. Government incentives often do much more or much less than expected. Profit-minded entrepreneurs exploit the government's largesse. Costs squeezed out of one place pop up elsewhere; save money by discouraging inpatient surgery and outpatient surgery costs skyrocket, for instance. And it is increasingly expensive. Adjusted for inflation, the federal government spent more on Medicare and Medicaid in 2011 than it spent on *everything* in 1960.

In 1968, Senator Kuchel was defeated in a primary by a more conservative Republican, and Panetta ended up in the Nixon administration overseeing federal efforts to force southern schools to desegregate in what was then the Department of Health, Education, and Welfare. The job lasted only fourteen months. Nixon's interest in courting the South conflicted with young Panetta's aggressiveness in enforcing the law. He was fired and wrote a book about the episode, *Bring Us Together*. The cover on one of the later printings identified him as "the man who blew the whistle on the Nixon administration two years before Watergate." After a stint working for New York mayor John Lindsay, he went home to practice law with his brother.

NIXON: CONGRESS STRIKES BACK

Among his other accomplishments (or transgressions), Richard Nixon antagonized Congress by refusing to spend billions of dollars that lawmakers had approved. In 1974, Congress struck back with the Congressional Budget Act, passed over Nixon's veto a month before he resigned. It created a congressional budget process parallel to the president-centric system created in FDR's time. New House and Senate budget committees were established to coordinate panels responsible for tax and spending bills, and a series of target dates for action each year was set to impose order on the process. The most durable innovation was the creation of the Congressional Budget Office, or CBO, which freed Congress from relying almost exclusively on economic forecasts and budget analysis from the White House budget office.

In recent years, the process envisioned in the 1974 law has broken down amid partisan discord. In 2010 and 2011, the two houses of Congress failed to agree on the mandated budget blueprint. Congress hasn't finished annual spending bills before the October 1 start to the fiscal year since 1998. But in a city riddled with dysfunctional institutions, the CBO has become one of the few organs of Congress that actually work. It is the arbiter of facts, a call-it-as-we-see-it outfit that is viewed as largely immune to political pressure.

When the CBO was conceived, the Senate imagined a high-powered think tank with a director, as then Senate Budget

Committee chairman Ed Muskie said, "who can grasp the dimensions of the global problem that this new committee is going to be struggling with." The House imagined something quite different. As Robert Reischauer, a former CBO director, once put it: "Congress would have a bill or something, and it would lift up the manhole cover and put the bill down it, and you would hear grinding noises, and 20 minutes later a piece of paper would be handed up with a cost estimate." It was, he said, "to be non-controversial the way the sewer system is."

The Senate won and, over the objections of some in the House, Alice Rivlin became the first director of the agency. Rivlin was a pioneer. Rejected by Harvard's graduate school of public administration, now the Kennedy School of Government, in the 1950s "on the explicit grounds that a woman of marriageable age was a 'poor risk,'" she turned to economics, then a field in which about 5 percent of Ph.D. students were female. "In retrospect, the amazing thing was that the women were not more outraged," she says. "I think we thought we were lucky to be there at all." Outwitting the system was kind of a game. One of the university libraries was closed to women, and its books could not even be borrowed for a female on inter-library loan. "I don't remember being upset. If I needed a book, I just got a male friend to check it out for me," she recalls. With academic tenure-track jobs largely closed to women, she spent her early career alternating between government (the Johnson-era Department of Health, Education, and Welfare) and think tanks (the Brookings Institution, which is largely populated by Democrats).

Rivlin is short in stature, less than five feet, but steely. She was determined to build an institution with influence and independence. At age eighty-one she remains an active and formidable advocate for fiscal rectitude, serving on blue-ribbon panels and appearing on public forums. With Muskie's backing, she built a staff independent of what she called the "schmoozy, good ol' boy Hill culture." While the CBO director job has alternated between Democrats and Republicans, the culture of nonpartisan analysis built by Rivlin and her Republican successor, Rudy Penner, has endured. Rivlin annoyed President Jimmy Carter with skepticism about his energy proposals. Reischauer, a Democrat, resisted Clinton White House pressure to avoid labeling as "taxes" rather than "premiums" the mandatory employer contributions to health insurance in Clinton's health plan. Douglas Holtz-Eakin disappointed his fellow Republicans who wanted the CBO to count more of the economic benefits of tax cuts when putting a price tag on them. When the current CBO director, Douglas Elmendorf, wouldn't vouch for Obama White House predictions of big savings from the president's health care reforms, Peter Orszag–the White House budget director who had preceded Elmendorf in the CBO post–protested publicly that his successor was "overstepping." For budget geeks, it was like the showdown at the O.K. Corral, albeit by dueling blog posts. "Elmendorf," businessman-turned-commentator RJ Eskow wrote in the *Huffington Post,* "is the stone-faced banker who won't lend the money, while Orszag's the inventor holding a prototype of the hula hoop."

This pressure on the CBO can actually encourage truth telling, says Holtz-Eakin. "In the end, everyone will always complain to you, so it gets easier to just tell the truth," he says. Congressmen want someone "to kick in public" but most value a scorekeeper that tries to be objective, he says. And even when they don't like the CBO's conclusions, members of Congress value the leverage the office gives Congress in its budget dustups with the White House.

"To a degree that may have been unforeseen when the 1974 act was formulated," University of Maryland budget maven Allen Schick says, "the new system institutionalized and expanded budgetary conflict." Eventually, the two branches have to agree on spending bills or the government shuts down. "But first," says Schick, "they fight... [not] over the details, as was once common, [but] over big policy matters—the size of government, defense versus domestic programs, how much total spending and revenues should rise... whether to cut the deficit by trimming expenditures or by boosting taxes, and so on."

THE REAGAN REVOLUTION:
THE BEAST IS NOT STARVED

In 1975, a year after the CBO was created, the budget hit a little-noticed milestone: for the first time, spending on interest, Social Security, Medicare, and other benefits exceeded the defense and domestic spending that Congress must approve annually. A year later, having become a Democrat, Panetta was elected to Congress from his hometown. Four years further on, fellow Californian Ronald Reagan was elected president.

The Reagan presidency was styled as a turning point in American politics: the end of the New Deal and the beginning of an era in which the government would retreat from the economy. Ronald Reagan made three significant fiscal promises during his campaign for president: cut taxes, rebuild the nation's defenses, and balance the budget. He delivered on the first two, but not on the third.

Later, the notion that cutting taxes would lead to compensating cuts in government spending became known as the "starve the beast" strategy, a phrase made famous by Daniel Patrick Moynihan, the late, erudite Democratic senator from New York. In his usual folksy style, Reagan lent credence to this theory in a February 1981 televised speech: "Well, you know, we can lecture our children about extravagance until we run out of voice and breath. Or we can cure their extravagance by simply reducing their allowance."

But insider accounts of the Reagan years describe a haphazard, almost chaotic process inside the White House. Some Reagan aides were committed to cutting spending, notably David Stockman, the Paul Ryan of his day. Elected to Congress at age thirty, Stockman left the House of Representatives after four years to become Reagan's budget director, determined to dismantle vast segments of the welfare state. "If you insisted on a balanced budget but accepted all the illicit welfare-state spending commitments that have been accumulated over the years . . . you became the tax collector for the welfare state," Stockman wrote in his memoir. He did not want that role.

Another group around Reagan, known as the supply-siders, argued that cutting tax rates would unleash a surge of economic activity from the producers in the economy. Within the White House, they derided Stockman and his allies as "root canal" Republicans determined to inflict the pain of spending cuts to pursue a misguided antipathy toward deficits.

One of the supply-siders, Jude Wanniski, a *Wall Street Journal* editorial writer, had popularized what he called the "Two Santa Claus Theory" in 1976: "The Democrats, the party of income redistribution, are best suited for the role of Spending Santa Claus. The Republicans, traditionally the party of income growth, should be the Santa Claus of Tax Reduction. It has been the failure of the GOP to stick to this traditional role that has caused much of the nation's economic misery. . . . It isn't that Republicans don't enjoy cutting taxes. They love it. But there is something in the Republican chemistry that causes the GOP to become hypnotized by the prospect of an imbalanced budget. . . . [T]hey embrace the role of Scrooge, playing into the hands of the Democrats, who know the first rule of successful politics is Never Shoot Santa Claus."

On spending, much of the Reagan cabinet and a good chunk of the Republican congressional leadership labored to shield their favorite programs from Stockman's knife. And they succeeded.

Even without the spending cuts, the Reagan tax cut passed in 1981. More than half the Democrats in the House voted for the bill, Panetta among them, despite his later criticism of it. He already had voted for a smaller tax cut, a compromise offered by Representative Dan Rostenkowski of Illinois, then the chairman of the tax-writing committee. But that bill had failed. "At that point," Panetta said in a recent interview, "I thought I'd been fighting [Reagan] on every front, and he was very popular in my district, and I said, you know, having voted for the Rostenkowski tax cut, I just find it very difficult to now turn around and suddenly vote against [the Reagan] tax cut. That's the scenario."

The Reagan tax cut was gigantic: its provisions, the Treasury estimated later, would have slashed federal revenues by 18 percent in the first two years. "If the American political system had acted the way it normally does, it would have lopped off the extremes and forced a compromise within moderate bounds," Richard Darman, a Reagan White House aide and later George H. W. Bush's budget director, recalled in his memoir. "But in this case, even as it became absolutely clear that necessary spending control would not be achieved, the system allowed a way-out-of-the-ordinary tax cut to become law."

Whatever the reasons—Darman later (and characteristically) offered a ten-point explanation—the result was the 1981 tax cut without the hoped-for spending cuts. Stockman famously predicted deficits of "$200 billion a year as far as the eye can see," numbers that sounded huge at the time. He was prescient. The 1980s broke a pattern in which the federal government ran big deficits only in wartime. The deficits topped $200 billion a year from 1983 through 1992. They would have been even bigger if Reagan hadn't flinched on taxes, accepting significant tax increases in 1982 and 1984.

Reagan enjoyed many victories as president. But starving the beast was not one of them. When he left office, federal spending was 20 percent higher, adjusted for inflation, than it had been when he arrived, and he never found a way to pay for it. In the twenty years before Reagan became president–under Kennedy, Johnson, Nixon, and Carter–the budget deficit averaged well under 1 percent of GDP. In Reagan's eight years, it averaged 4.25 percent of GDP.

Panetta summed up Reaganomics in a single sentence: "A significant tax cut was enacted at the same time that defense spending went up and . . . entitlement programs were also expanding." When Reagan turned the presidency over to George H. W. Bush, the deficit was 2.8 percent of GDP–and rising.

THE ARRIVAL OF SURPLUSES:
READING GEORGE H. W. BUSH'S LIPS

Bush was elected in 1988 with one memorable promise: "Read my lips, no new taxes." Republican pollster Richard Wirthlin once called them "the six most destructive words in the history of presidential politics."

When Bush assumed the presidency, Panetta was chairman of the House Budget Committee, the panel created in the 1974 reforms of the budget process. From that perch, he decried "a borrow, bailout, and buy-out binger that pervades our society and puts our future economic security at risk," warning further—in phrases that are heard again today—that "our capacity to govern" was being tested.

"Both Democrats and Republicans talked about reducing this deficit, but neither wanted an approach to touch their favorite programs," he recalled years later. "The Republicans said they would balance the budget, but they did not want to raise taxes, and they did not want to cut defense. The Democrats, on the other hand, said, 'We want to balance the budget, but we don't want to cut domestic programs, we don't want to reduce any entitlement programs. What we want to do is reduce defense and raise taxes.'

"So," Panetta went on, "the very areas that had to be part of a solution were the areas that both parties staked out as holy territory that couldn't be touched. That created the dilemma." He was talking about 1990, but he could just as easily have been talking about 2012.

About eighteen months after taking the oath of office, George H. W. Bush ate his words. In June 1990, after a two-hour breakfast at the White House with congressional leaders from both parties, Bush's press office issued a statement: "It is clear to me"—the last two words were inserted at the insistence of the Senate Democratic leader, George Mitchell—"that both the size of the deficit problem and the need for a package that can be enacted require all of the following. . . ." The laundry list that followed included the politically salient phrase "tax revenue increases."

After three torturous months of negotiations, much of it at Andrews Air Force Base outside Washington, Richard Darman and the president's other advisers cut a deal with Panetta and the congressional Democrats, who had a majority in Congress. Newt Gingrich, then the number two House Republican, led a rebellion—and the deal was rejected by the House. After three weeks, a new deal was cut. To woo more Democratic votes, tax rates on the rich were pushed higher than in the original agreement.

"The American people have had enough of [being told] that somehow we can confront the deficit and it doesn't involve pain," Panetta told a reporter at the time. "The fact is that it does." The final deal cut spending by $2 for every $1 of tax increases and, to the consternation of some Republicans, raised the top marginal income tax rate (the levy on each additional dollar of income) to 31 percent from 28 percent, the level to which it had been lowered in the Tax Reform Act of 1986.

The vote tally for the 1990 deal underscores just how much Congress has changed. A Republican president relied on a majority of House Democrats (181 yes and 47 no) to overcome the opposition of a majority of House Republicans (74 yes and 126 no) to raise taxes and cut spending. Today, the idea that a president could appeal to a mixed-party center to win approval of any measure seems as quaint as a typewriter.

"For Democrats during that period, with Republican presidents, we made the fundamental decision that governing was good politics for us [in terms of] maintaining our power," Panetta recalled recently with the hindsight of more than twenty years. "I don't get a sense today that either side thinks that governing is necessarily good politics."

The law did cut the deficit from what it otherwise would have been—a concept always easier for economists to grasp than the public—but still the deficit grew. The economy deteriorated, revenues fell short of projections, and spending on Medicare and Medicaid rose faster than anticipated. Rising deficits tarnished the image of a compromise born of a broken presidential promise. Bush later told TV interviewer Barbara Walters that the deal was "a mistake because it undermined to some degree my credibility with the American people." But he insisted it hadn't hurt the economy. Republicans often suggest otherwise and even today blame the deal for triggering a recession that began three months before it passed Congress. Darman, who died in 2008, blamed the recession on the Fed for not cutting interest rates quickly enough.

From the vantage point of twenty years, the evidence favors those who say the deal restrained deficits from what they otherwise would have been. "The record shows that the 1990 budget deal was extremely effective in reducing deficits; the budget surpluses of the late 1990s owe much to the policies put in place by George H. W. Bush that his son and party later repudiated," says Bruce Bartlett, a veteran of the Reagan and first

Bush administrations who has become a critic of Republican fiscal policy.

Beyond the important details of spending and taxes, the 1990 deal made two significant changes:

It established a pay-as-you-go rule that made it hard for Congress to cut taxes or increase benefits without offsetting tax increases or spending cuts. For more than a decade, this rule restrained Congress from significant expansion of government benefits. A decade later, when this rule lapsed, Congress and the president did exactly what the rule sought to avoid: expanded Medicare to cover prescription drugs without funding the new program.

After bumping up spending in the first year to buy congressional backing for the deal, the 1990 agreement also set multiyear caps on annual appropriations for the first time. Congress was, essentially, tying its own hands, or at least promising to do so. In one sense, the caps held. Adjusted for inflation, annually appropriated spending in 1996 was 13 percent below the 1990 level. But the total masks a key factor: "The Soviet Union fell apart, and there was no justification for such a huge military," says Bob Reischauer. In 1990, outlays for defense were $300 billion, and outlays for domestic programs subject to annual appropriations were $200 billion. Six years later, they were even at $266 billion each.

The 1990 deal was only a down payment, though. Debate over how much the government should spend and on what continued. "I think the most dangerous threat to our national security right now is debt, very heavy debt, that we confront in this country," Panetta, then House Budget Committee chairman, lectured then defense secretary Richard B. Cheney and General Colin L. Powell, the chairman of the Joint Chiefs of Staff, at a 1992 hearing. "I don't question anything you're saying in terms of the role that this country ought to perform. My problem is how the hell are we going to pay for it?"

Shortly after Bill Clinton was elected, he invited Panetta to Little Rock, Arkansas, where the president-elect was organizing his administration. "We talked a long time about the deficit, and, frankly, the campaign in '92. Ross Perot [the Texas businessman who ran as a third-party candidate] had made the deficit a major issue of that campaign, which helped a great deal, ultimately, in trying to confront it." Clinton's advisers were split between those who wanted to reduce the deficit first and those who wanted to deliver on the campaign's promise of increasing federal investments. The cut-the-deficit-first crowd won. Among its members were Panetta, who became Clinton's budget director, and Rivlin, who became Panetta's deputy and later his successor, and Robert Rubin, who would become Clinton's White House economic-policy coordinator and later Treasury secretary. They convinced Clinton to ditch his campaign promises to cut taxes for the middle class and sharply increase government investment spending and, instead, to focus on bringing down the deficit.

After substantial haggling–and an energy tax that was abandoned by the White House–Clinton's deficit-reduction bill, heavier on tax increases than spending cuts, got through Congress. In striking contrast to 1990, every Republican in the House and Senate opposed it. Vice President Al Gore broke a tie in the Senate, and last-minute pressure on reluctant Democrats produced a 218–216 vote in the House in 1993. One of the last Democrats to vote for the bill was Marjorie Margolies-Mezvinsky, a first-term congresswoman from Philadelphia's suburbs who had previously said she would oppose the bill. Her vote was later blamed for her defeat in 1994. (Clinton's daughter later married her son.)

The deal extended the 1990 limits on annual appropriated spending through 1998, squeezed payments to health care providers, and raised taxes, primarily on upper-income taxpayers. This time the deficit-reduction effort worked as promised. The deficit came down even faster than the CBO projected as the economy picked up momentum and incomes of the rich—whose taxes had been raised by the law—rose sharply. In 1995, the IRS counted 87,000 returns with incomes of more than $1 million, up from 66,500 in 1993. These millionaires saw their incomes rise by $57 billion over those two years, and they paid $18 billion more income taxes.

Republicans gave Clinton no credit for the shrinking deficit. At one unusually testy appearance before the House committee he had once chaired, Panetta, then White House budget director, exploded under questioning from Olympia Snowe, a moderate and mild-mannered Republican from Maine. "You know," he said, "does it really hurt that much to admit that we are impacting on the deficit? Does it really hurt that much to say that we are going in the right direction? Does it really hurt that much to give us a little credit for what we are try-ing to do ... ?" Even for those familiar with Panetta's behind-the-scenes outbursts, the harsh words were startling, a display of frustration and a reminder that partisanship over budgets is hardly a recent phenomenon. A few minutes later, Panetta apologized: "Sometimes the Italian part of me gets in control of my emotions."

In the 1994 elections, Republicans took the House for the first time in four decades, their campaign aided by their at-tacks on Democrats for raising taxes in 1993. Newt Gingrich became the speaker. Emboldened Republicans confronted Clinton over spending, producing two government shutdowns before agreement was reached. After a couple of years as Clin-ton's chief of staff, Panetta went home. He sounded bitter. "In the time that I've been in Washington politics has gotten meaner ... where instead of spending time talking about the broader issues–on education, welfare reform, health care, and what have you ... it's become much, much more of a political temptation ... to grab that 30-second spot on the evening news to engage in this kind of attack politics." Referring to Repub-licans, he said, "I honestly think they're losing points with the American public, but ... there's still a mentality that if they can score the first punch, that somehow that benefits them."

Two years after Gingrich led the Republican takeover of the House, Bill Clinton went to Capitol Hill to deliver his 1996

State of the Union address, and sounded a Reaganesque theme: "We know big government does not have all the answers. We know there's not a program for every problem. . . . The era of big government is over." Republicans cheered. Clinton and Gingrich had economic winds at their back—a strengthening economy, a rising stock market, soaring incomes in the top tax brackets. Suddenly, a balanced budget appeared to be within reach. In 1997, Gingrich and Clinton—with Panetta's successor as chief of staff, Erskine Bowles, doing much of the negotiating—reached a deal to cut taxes but restrain spending more, at least on paper. One money saver would later become a headache, though. The deal legislated unrealistically large cuts to fees Medicare pays doctors in the future; in later years, Congress would waive the cuts regularly.

The pact marked a high-water mark in recent cooperation on budgets between Republicans and Democrats. From the Obama White House in 2012, Jack Lew reflected almost wistfully on the 1990s: "Leon [Panetta] and John Kasich [the Ohio congressman who was the senior Republican on the House Budget Committee] would get in a room and scream at each other. It was awkward to be in the room sometimes. But at the end of the day, they could do business together. You go through that, and you do business together."

Emboldened by their success, Clinton and Gingrich flirted with a once-in-a-generation fix to Social Security so its finances could withstand the retirement of the baby boomers.

But Clinton's dalliance with intern Monica Lewinsky and the impeachment trial that followed destroyed any chance of a grand bargain between the president and Congress. "Gingrich wanted to do it; Clinton wanted to do it. It was a real missed opportunity," Bowles says. "Monica changed everything."

Lew and the deficit-fearing contingents in both parties look at the Reagan tax increases of the 1980s and the Bush deficit deal of 1990 as the good old days, and keep searching for ways to re-create the politics that spawned those compromises. Paul Ryan and the small-government, antitax slice of the Republican Party see them as evils to be avoided because they reduced the deficit without permanently shrinking the government. "Why would we go back to the '82 and '90 deals where we put taxes on the table, and we didn't get spending cuts?" says Grover Norquist, the influential antitax crusader and strategist.

THE RETURN OF DEFICITS: TAX CUTS, WARS, AND PRESCRIPTION DRUGS

For four years, 1998 through 2001, the federal government ran surpluses, a remarkable development that put deficit worrywarts nearly out of business and made all the warnings about rising health care costs and the approaching retirement of the baby boomers much less threatening. As a presidential candidate, George W. Bush promised to tap the surpluses to cut taxes. Federal Reserve chairman Alan Greenspan, at the time the most credible economist in the country, widely hailed as *the* voice of fiscal rectitude, was called to the Senate Budget Committee in January 2001 to testify. As is the custom, the Fed sent an advance copy of the written testimony to the committee. Kent Conrad, the fiscally conservative Democrat who chaired the committee, read it–and winced. "[T]he highly desirable goal of paying off the federal debt is in reach before the end of the decade," Greenspan said. The money would burn a hole in the government's pocket: if taxes weren't cut, it would be spent. Greenspan favored tax cuts, and said so, with carefully worded qualifications that he could point to later but few heard at the time.

Conrad called Greenspan to his office and told him his words would trigger "a feeding frenzy." He made no headway and asked Bob Rubin, the former Treasury secretary, to call. Rubin was no more successful. Greenspan delivered the testimony as written and got precisely the reaction that Conrad and Rubin had foreseen. The headline in the next morning's *Wall Street Journal* said, "Greenspan, in About-Face, Backs Tax Cuts." In his 2007 memoir, Greenspan allowed that he had "misjudged the emotions of the moment." The most prescient part of his testimony was little noted at the time: an admonition against "policies that could readily resurrect the deficits of the past." Indeed, 2001 would be the last year that Washington ran a surplus.

WHERE DID THE SURPLUSES GO?

In January 2001, the CBO, then headed by Dan Crippen, a burly, bearded former aide to Ronald Reagan, issued the annual ten-year budget projections to which Greenspan referred. If current policies continued and the economy, which was weakening at the time, rebounded as anticipated, the United States would run budget *surpluses* each year from 2002 through 2011. Collectively, these surpluses would total $5.6 trillion, enough to pay off the entire federal debt, according to the CBO.

In January 2012, the CBO, now headed by a slender, bearded economist who had worked for Bill Clinton, Doug Elmendorf, issued another ten-year update. The tables in the back showed that from 2002 to 2011, the government had run *deficits* each year. The total: $6.1 trillion worth of deficits over ten years.

How did those surpluses turn into deficits? How could the CBO be off by nearly $12 trillion, an astounding sum? The short answers: a lousier than anticipated economy, some big tax cuts, two wars that weren't paid for, an expansion of Medicare to cover prescription drugs that wasn't paid for, and—later—the damage done by the worst recession since the Great Depression.

Let's take them one at a time.

First, the economy did worse than the CBO and most other forecasters anticipated. The dot-com bubble burst, precipitating the recession of the early 2000s, which was compounded by the shock of the September 2001 terrorist attacks. The recession was mild and the economy recovered. But the hits kept coming: first the housing bubble burst, then the financial crisis hit, and the Great Recession was on. That hurt revenues—fewer capital gains, fewer profits, and fewer jobs mean less tax revenue to the Treasury. And it increased spending because more people were eligible for government unemployment, food stamps, and health benefits.

Net from economy: $3.3 trillion.

Two, Congress cut taxes—repeatedly. The big one was George W. Bush's 2001 tax cut, enacted at a moment when there was genuine concern about the prospect that government might run such persistent surpluses that it would pay off all its debt, which would have raised such unfamiliar problems as a shortage of Treasury debt for financial markets to trade. The first Bush tax cut reduced revenues by about $1.2 trillion over ten years, according to the CBO. Smaller tax cuts followed over the years, and then came the ones that Obama pushed to fight the deep recession that was afflicting the country when he was sworn in.

Net from tax cuts: $2.8 trillion.

Three, the government spent more—a lot more. The cost of the wars in Afghanistan and Iraq came to roughly $1.2 trillion over the decade, and there was extra spending on homeland security after 9/11. The expansion of Medicare to cover prescription drugs cost about $275 billion just through 2011. The much-criticized Troubled Asset Relief Program, which was used to bail out the banks, and the Obama-backed stimulus package added another $500 billion through 2011, but much of that was later recouped as banks paid off their loans.

Net from spending: $4.3 trillion.

Four, bigger deficits mean more borrowing. In January 2001, CBO projections anticipated that the entire federal debt would be paid off by now, which would have meant no interest costs. Instead, the debt held by the public—everyone from the Chinese government to the savings bonds in American desk drawers, but excluding the Social Security trust fund—stood at $10 trillion. And more borrowing means an ever-larger interest tab.

Net increase in the deficit from interest: $1.4 trillion.

In the late 1990s and early 2000s, chief executives of corporations became celebrity heroes, and politicians seemed increasingly irrelevant amid the centrifugal force of the Internet. The pace of federal spending increases slowed, and the reforms to which Clinton and Gingrich had agreed pushed many from welfare to work as the economy boomed. Then the stock market plunged, chief executives became celebrity crooks, and the September 11, 2001, attacks shattered the notion that with the

Cold War over, the market could cope with nearly everything. Despite Clinton's State of the Union declaration, government grew, again. "The era of big government wasn't over," said Allen Schick, the Maryland professor. "Look at what happened with spending. It was hibernating under Clinton and revived under Bush."

Once in office, George W. Bush delivered on his campaign promise to cut taxes. His first tax cut, in 2001, was smaller than Reagan's but was followed by additional tax cuts the following four years that collectively exceeded Reagan's. Simultaneously, most of the spending restraints written into his father's 1990 deficit deal expired. Then, at the end of Bush's first year in office, his presidency was redefined by the 9/11 terror attacks, and so was the federal budget. Two wars and intensified efforts at homeland security increased spending significantly. In 2001, defense spending was 3 percent of GDP, half the Reagan-era peak. In 2011, it was 5 percent. (Each percentage point of GDP is about $150 billion.)

Bush also signed into law the first significant expansion of Medicare in forty years. When Medicare was designed in the 1960s, prescription drugs weren't a big part of health care so the program didn't cover most drugs. By the first decade of the twenty-first century, they accounted for 12 percent of all personal health care spending, and pressure to expand Medicare to cover them was intense. The drug insurance program created in 2003 was built around two elements of lasting consequence to the budget: One, the government would subsidize the purchase of competing private drug insurance policies and wouldn't negotiate directly with drug companies. And, two, no attempt was made to pay for the bill. The only constraint was an agreement to limit the tab to $400 billion over ten years, even though everyone knew it would cost more in the future. By 2010, the *annual* tab exceeded $60 billion, about $1 of every $8 in Medicare outlays. Government actuaries projected the cost would climb nearly 10 percent a year in the following decade.

Obama summed this up in an April 2011 speech at George Washington University: "[A]fter Democrats and Republicans committed to fiscal discipline during the 1990s, we lost our way in the decade that followed. We increased spending dramatically for two wars and an expensive prescription drug program—but we didn't pay for any of this new spending. Instead, we made the problem worse with trillions of dollars in unpaid-for tax cuts."

A year before the 2008 election that would bring Leon Panetta back to Washington—and before the Great Recession had hit—he and a few other veterans of the 1990s deficit wars were called by Kent Conrad to appear before the Senate Budget Committee. Panetta had been out of government for years, building a public policy institute in Monterey. He came to Washington periodically to scold his successors in his role as cochairman of the Committee for a Responsible Federal Budget, a hardy antideficit lobby that brings together aging budget experts from both parties to wring their hands and offer advice, welcomed or not.

In congressional testimony, Panetta recalled the surpluses that the government had been running when he left Washington. He remembered hoping that his successors "would never again permit runaway deficits to undermine [the nation's] economic strength." But, he said sternly, "events, partisanship, and a failure of leadership on all sides have conspired to produce the kind of irresponsible fiscal behavior that again threatens our future."

The combination of "exploding" benefit programs, the aging of the population, the "rapid rise" in health care costs, and growing interest payments "places us on an unsustainable path to fiscal chaos.

"What is even more discouraging," he said, with a sigh, "is that it ignores virtually everything we have learned the hard way in the past."

CHAPTER 3

WHERE THE MONEY GOES

The federal budget is as vast as the government itself: the instructions the White House sends agencies for making and keeping track of annual budget requests run 972 pages. The *instructions*. The four-volume budget that Obama sent to Congress in February 2012 came to 2,238 pages. Then each agency produced thousands of pages of more detail. The Department of Homeland Security's supplement topped out at 3,134 pages, one page for every $12.6 million it was seeking to spend.

To make sense of all this, groups that promote fiscal rectitude have boiled the budget down to (relatively) simple online games: cut spending here, raise taxes there, and see if you can do better at bringing the deficit under control than Congress and the president. There's *Stabilize the Debt* by the Committee for a Responsible Federal Budget and *Federal Budget Challenge* by the Concord Coalition. The most elaborate is *Budget Hero,* built by educational gamers for the Woodrow Wilson International Center for Scholars, a government-backed Washington think tank, and American Public Media, a public radio network. This is no *Call of Duty* or *Portal 2*. There's no adrenaline rush from deciding whose taxes to raise or how much to cut the defense budget. But since it was launched on the Web in 2008, *Budget Hero* has been played 1.4 million times. The game plucks options from the thick catalog of ways to reduce the deficit published annually by the Congressional Budget Office and puts them into a Pokémon-style video game. Just as in real life, there is no single goal. Players identify up to three objectives, such as achieving greater energy independence or improving the competitiveness of the U.S. economy, and try to use the spending and tax levers to reach them. A running tally shows the consequences of their choices on deficits and the size of government. The overarching lesson: Bringing the deficit down to sustainable levels takes big changes. Little ones won't do it.

Despite the video games and think tank websites and newspaper pie charts and televised presidential debates, the public remains strikingly misinformed about the budget. The typical respondent to a CNN poll said food stamps accounted for 10 percent of federal spending; it's closer to 2 percent. Maybe being off by a factor of five is understandable given the enormity and complexity of the budget. But it's harder to make sense of a 2008 Cornell University poll in which 44 percent of those who receive Social Security checks and 40 percent of those covered by Medicare say they "have not used a government social program."

Polls also find that Americans cling to the belief that government is a sea of waste and inefficiency that can be excised painlessly. When Gallup asked last year how much of each tax dollar sent to Washington is wasted, the answer averaged *51 cents*, the highest since the polling outfit began posing the question in 1979. Yes, the federal government harbors gobs of waste and inefficiency–the Department of Homeland Security recently discovered it was spending $10.6 million on unused wireless devices–but the public overstates the magnitude. Reports on government corruption also reinforce this idea, even when the underhanded dealings ultimately cost taxpayers very little. For example, the *Washington Post* identified thirty-three members of Congress who quietly steered government grants to road improvement and other projects near pieces of private property they owned. The tab: $300 million, less than one hour's worth of federal spending. Nonetheless, every president vows to pare waste, fraud, abuse, and inefficiency, but the budgetary relief is often underwhelming. The Obama budget boasted that the Social Security Administration took an employee suggestion to use e-mail instead of snail mail to distribute commemorative flyers to its offices nine times a year. The grand total saved: $5,000 a year.

"Reducing the deficit by cutting 'waste, fraud, and abuse' never works: there's seldom any agreement on what qualifies as waste," says Stan Collender, a Washington public relations man who has built a business explaining the federal budget to outsiders. "Everyone thinks there's a lot, but there's nothing that a majority wants to cut. The average person doesn't want less government. They just want the government to cost less."

MERGE WITH CANADA

Rob Portman, a Republican U.S. senator from Ohio and George W. Bush's White House budget director, understands the politics of persuading constituents that they are going to have to give up something to bring down the deficit. So when he was named to a congressional deficit-reduction committee last year, he asked Ohioans to offer *their* suggestions on his website. "My goal was to actually end up taking some of these and being able to say, here's something that came from Joe Smith in Akron, Ohio," he said. "And we would have been able to do that had we come up with something [a committee agreement] because a number of their ideas were part of the mix."

Not all of the ideas were practical: a constituent from Cincinnati suggested that the United States merge with Canada, while someone from Columbia Station advocated replacing paid congressional staff with volunteers. Others were sober and serious: JZ from Cincinnati suggested raising the age at which Americans qualify for Social Security and Medicare. A farmer from Lebanon proposed paring farm subsidies. CM from Bay Village questioned the merits of allowing holders of municipal

Where the Money Goes

In 2011, Social Security, Medicare, Medicaid, and other benefits accounted for about 56% of all federal spending. Defense took about 20% and interest about 6%. That left 18% for everything else.

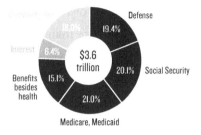

Source: White House Office of Management and Budget

The Age of Entitlements

Social Security, Medicare, Medicaid, and other benefits known as "entitlements" represent a growing share of all federal spending over the past fifty years. Annually appropriated spending, especially for defense, is a shrinking share.

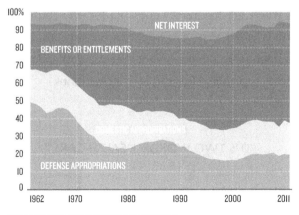

Source: White House Office of Management and Budget

bonds to avoid federal taxes on the interest they earn. Even the feasible ones, though, amounted to nibbling at the edges.

When Portman tries to explain the budget to constituents, he slices it into several pieces: "One is the annually appropriated spending that gets all of the attention. But when you take out defense, which is more than half of it, it ends up being 18 percent of the budget. Then you've got defense spending . . . that's the second big part.

"And the third big part—and the fast-growing part—is the mandatory spending," he continues, lapsing into Washington jargon for benefits paid to those eligible without any annual vote by Congress. "You can divide that into basically three things: It's interest. It's Social Security. It's the health care programs, Medicare and Medicaid."

The federal budget can be sliced in any number of ways. Portman's are as good as any. But his slices are huge, and each has many parts, subparts, and individual programs. So to get a feel for where all that money goes and for why cutting spending sounds easier than it is, slice the budget into five pieces besides interest—health care, Social Security, other benefits, defense, and everything else—and take a closer look.

"IT'S TWO WORDS: HEALTH CARE"

"When I left OMB in 2007," Portman said in an interview, "people asked me: 'What did you learn? What's the biggest

The Doctor Bill

Government spending on health care, mainly the Medicare and Medicaid insurance programs, is the fastest-growing major piece of the budget, accounting now for more than a quarter of all federal spending.

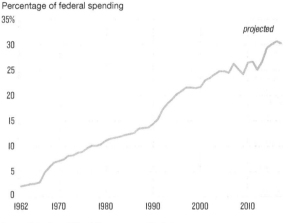

Percentage of federal spending

Source: White House Office of Management and Budget

concern about our budget? Is it the spending in Iraq and Afghanistan? Is it tax revenues? Is it the spending?'

"I said, 'No. It's two words: health care.'"

The numbers support that assessment. Health care spending is rising faster than any other major part of the federal budget, driven by a costly trio of factors. One, the number of insured is rapidly increasing as Congress expands the pool of those who are eligible, fewer people get health insurance on the job, and the huge baby boom generation turns sixty-five and becomes eligible for Medicare. Two, those insured through government-subsidized insurance are using more health care, undergoing more procedures, and availing themselves of new technologies. Three, the price of that health care is rising faster than the price of other goods and services.

These three facts add up to a predictable and alarming trend: already expensive, health care is likely to balloon in cost in coming years. Medicare for the elderly and disabled and Medicaid for the poor currently account for about 21 percent of all federal spending. Medicare alone cost $555 billion in 2011; adjusted for inflation, that's more than the federal government spent on *everything* in 1951. The CBO forecasts that the Medicare tab will climb by 75 percent over the next decade. "It is the aging of the population and the rising costs of health care that are putting this unbearable pressure on the federal budget," CBO director Doug Elmendorf told Congress recently.

Replacing worn-out hip joints, a marvel of modern medicine that makes old age more comfortable, illustrates the three drivers of Medicare costs. First, more people are living longer, creating a larger pool of potential hips to be replaced. Second, the overall number of eligible patients electing the procedure is on the rise. Between 1999 and 2009, the number of hip replacements performed on patients between sixty-five and eighty-four rose 30 percent, and in a remarkable development, the number done on people over eighty-five rose 21 percent. By 2009, nearly one in every six Americans who had a hip joint replaced was over eighty-five. A generation or two earlier, it was next to none. Third, the cost per procedure has escalated.

In 2009, Medicare spent $9 billion replacing hip, knee, and shoulder joints, a tab that has been rising at better than

8 percent a year, with about a third of that going to 264,000 hip replacements at roughly $12,000 apiece. The Government Accountability Office, the investigative arm of Congress, estimates that while 40 percent of the increase in Medicare spending on hip replacements between 2004 and 2009 reflects the increase in the number of procedures, fully 60 percent is due to the rising cost per case.

Surveys of patients after surgery suggest that most are very satisfied, reporting an improved ability to walk and, in some cases, exercise or play sports, so the money may be well spent. But the popularity of the procedure is also an ominous portent for Medicare's finances: the rapid adoption of joint replacement among middle-aged, non-Medicare-covered Americans is growing, and those artificial hips don't last forever. When it's time to replace them, the patients are likely to be of Medicare age.

The upward pressure on costs is not just a result of more and pricier procedures. The way the government pays for health care is itself a patchwork of perverse incentives crafted for reasons historical and political. Among these costly legacies is a decades-old embrace of fee-for-service, an approach to paying for medical care that tends to encourage more, but not necessarily better, care. In dozens of ways, the cost problem is exacerbated by the way that the government goes about paying for health care.

Consider just one example. Before Congress expanded Medicare to cover prescription drugs in 2003, the most impoverished of the elderly–about 16 percent of the aged–got drug coverage through Medicaid, the joint state and federal government health insurance program for the poor. By law, pharmaceutical companies must charge Medicaid the lower of "the best price" they charge anyone for a drug, or a price 15 percent below a benchmark. That saves Medicaid a lot of money.

In 2003, however, Congress ended that practice. It shifted those low-income elderly whose pharmacy bills have been covered by Medicaid coverage to the new Medicare pharmaceutical program. But, reflecting the enthusiasm for markets over government, the new program was somewhat different. Under the new system, the elderly purchase drug insurance at government-subsidized prices from one of several competing private plans, and then the insurers–not the government–pay the drug tab. For low-income elderly, the change didn't cost them much; the government still picks up nearly all the cost. They account for about 40 percent of the people in the drug program, but because they tend to have multiple chronic conditions, they account for 56 percent of the program's current spending.

One aspect of this shift from one government drug plan to another turned out to be a boon for Big Pharma, as major drug companies are known, but expensive for taxpayers. The "best price" rule no longer applied. Drug insurers, the theory went, would negotiate with the drug companies and keep drug costs down. In general, this competition has worked better than naysayers expected. But for low-income elderly, the law put a lot of restraints on the insurance companies. They had, for instance, to cover every available drug for certain conditions for these beneficiaries. That limited their negotiating power with the drug companies and, thus, boosted the cost of the insurance. The bottom line: the government ended up paying more for drugs for the elderly poor than it did under the old system. How much more? That's confidential. A couple of Harvard economists dissected drug corporation financial statements and estimated that for one big drug company, this single feature of the Medicare drug insurance program increased revenues by 8 percent in 2006 over the previous year. The White House budget office estimates that reimposing the "best price" rule on drugs used by low-income elderly would save the government $155 billion over ten years. An open question: Would that come out of drug-company profits or would the companies simply raise prices on other drugs to compensate or cut back on research?

FEEDING THE FARMERS—AND THE KIDS

Although retirement and health care are among the very biggest federal programs, about 17 cents of every federal tax dollar goes to a wide range of other benefits, from veterans' benefits to farm subsidies. These diverse financial arrangements have one thing in common: at the end of the pipeline is some American who is getting a check or a promise. Most are convinced they deserve the money.

The federal government has been sending checks to farmers, in good times and bad, for eighty years. This began with a disastrous drop in farm prices in the late 1920s and the 1930s that prompted Herbert Hoover and Franklin Roosevelt to use government muscle and taxpayer money to boost farm prices—a supposedly temporary measure. The political appeal was obvious: more than 20 percent of the labor force at that time worked on farms and more than 40 percent of Americans lived in a rural area. Eighty years later, fewer than 2 percent of Americans make their living on the farm, and not even one in six lives in a rural area. Yet big farms have considerable clout and those "temporary" farm subsidies live on, accounting for about $15 billion in federal spending annually. About a third of the money comes in "direct payments," no-strings-attached checks that the government sends farmers.

Like many other benefit programs, farm subsidies are hard to unravel—a maze of payments, loans, and insurance that bewilders everyone except those who benefit from them, those who attack them, and those in Congress who craft them. Farm bills also include a unique mechanism that forces Congress to act: if it doesn't pass the bills that arise every four or five years on time, or extend the last one temporarily, the clock is turned back and government payments to farms are based on the unusually high crop prices of 1910 and 1914, adjusted for all the inflation that's occurred since then. Not surprisingly, the farm bill is one that Congress *always* finishes on time, or at least extends temporarily.

Despite their political support, these subsidies have occasionally come under fire. "When Republicans seized Congress in 1994, promising a revolutionary age of fiscal conservatism and free-market capitalism," *Time* magazine's Michael Grunwald wrote, "they vowed to gut command-and-coddle farm policies that they compared to Soviet communism. They wanted the government to treat agriculture like any other business, and they said they'd offer farmers a deal . . . farmers could plant what they wanted, but no more subsidies."

To that end, the 1996 Freedom to Farm Act severed some long-standing links between the subsidies farmers receive, the crops they grow, and the prices they get for them. For what was supposed be a five-year transition, the bill offered farmers $5 billion a year in direct payments.

The revolution didn't last but the new "temporary" payouts did. Sixteen years later, about $5 billion in direct-payment checks are still being written annually even as the farm economy booms. These payments are based on an arcane formula tied to what was grown on the land years ago, no matter what crops–if any–are grown on the land now. Because the payment rights transfer with these specific plots, real estate prices are boosted–even on land that has never been cultivated by the current owners. Journalist Dan Morgan calls the payments "an entitlement tied to ownership of land–a construct that some would associate more with 19th-century Prussia than 21st-century America." Half of the direct payments go to farmers with incomes above $100,000.

An example: the first congressional district in western Kansas has received more money in direct payments over the years than any other, $250 million in 2010, most of that to wheat, corn, and sorghum growers. As is true nationally, most of the money goes to a small set of big farmers: half of the money went to 5,000 of the district's 675,000 residents, according to a database cultivated by the Environmental Working Group. The top ten farms got more than $200,000 apiece. Obama's latest budget proposes to eliminate direct payments altogether, describing them as "no longer defensible." Even Tim Huelskamp, a Tea Party Republican and fifth-generation farmer who represents the district, isn't defending direct payments any longer. "Everybody needs to share," Huelskamp told a few dozen townsfolk gathered at the Graham County Courthouse recently. "If you're a farmer like me, you're going to expect less. Something's going to go away. The direct payments are going to go away."

But even if they do, the farmers in Huelskamp's district aren't worried about being cut off entirely. Many figure what they lose in direct payments they'll make up in increased federal subsidies for crop insurance, which covers losses caused by drought, floods, pests, and low market prices or yields. The government pays private insurers to run the program and pays about 60 percent of premium cost. The annual tab to the taxpayer: $10 billion, and growing.

At the other end of this subsidized-production tunnel are those who get government help to buy food. In one 2012 Republican presidential debate, Newt Gingrich derided Barack Obama as "the food-stamp president" and asserted, "More people have been put on food stamps by Barack Obama than any president in American history." Echoing the charge, Mitt Romney said that Obama "wants us to become an entitlement society where the people in this country feel they're all entitled to something from government, and where government takes from some to give to others."

Actually, even before Obama was elected, the government had expanded the program, offering food stamps to more people and making benefits more generous. Then the terrible economy pushed the income of additional Americans down to levels that qualified them for help. The 2009 Obama-backed stimulus made even more people eligible (more unemployed adults without kids, for instance), increased benefits, and gave states money to spread the word about the benefits. But what Gingrich didn't mention was that as of December 2011, fewer people had been added to the food stamp rolls in the first three years of Obama's presidency (14.5 million) than in the expansion of the program during George W. Bush's two terms (14.7 million).

Still, Gingrich was shining a spotlight on a big target. At the end of 2011, more than 46 million Americans were using food stamps, one in every seven people. (The stamps have now been replaced by a debit card good for an average of $285 a month per household for food, but not cigarettes or alcohol.)

Like so much of today's federal safety net, the origins of the food stamp program date to the Great Depression, eight decades ago. And like so many federal benefit programs, its longevity reflects the interests both of the people who benefit (the hungry) and of the industry (farming) that provides it. The administrator of the 1939 precursor to today's food stamps, Milo Perkins, put it clearly: "We got a picture of a gorge, with farm surpluses on one cliff and undernourished city folks with outstretched hands on the other. We set out to find a practical way to build a bridge across the chasm."

When food surpluses evaporated during World War II, the program died. After several unsuccessful attempts, the program was revived in 1964, partly due to the efforts of farm-state legislators George McGovern, Democrat of South Dakota, and Bob Dole, Republican of Kansas. Since then, Congress has tweaked the program repeatedly. In 1973, it allowed Alaskans to use food stamps to buy hunting and fishing equipment, though not guns or ammunition. Since the 1960s, as the *New York Times* put it, "the food stamp program has swung between seasons of bipartisan support and conservative attack." The farm lobby generally embraced it, while Ronald Reagan derided it and Bill Clinton's 1996 welfare reform bill tightened eligibility. A 2008 farm bill, which George Bush unsuccessfully vetoed for other reasons, made food stamps easier to get. As welfare recipients were pushed to go to work, the program was recast–at least until Gingrich's diatribe–not as "welfare," but as a way to aid those working at wages so low they're below or not far above the official poverty line.

Advocates for the poor say the expanding program has

made severe hunger in America rare. Paul Ryan, the House Republican point man on budgets, sees the expansion as just another example of "relentless and unsustainable growth" in federal benefits that should be reversed. The program cost the government $78 billion in 2011, about 40 percent more than the cost of the entire Department of Homeland Security, from the Coast Guard to antiterrorist intelligence agents stationed abroad.

As the economy heals and more people get jobs, the number of Americans on food stamps will fall, but the program is likely to remain a flash point as the need to reduce deficits puts benefits of all sorts under scrutiny. Ryan has proposed turning administration of the program over to the states, capping federal spending so that states aren't encouraged to recruit beneficiaries for a program that Washington finances, and imposing time limits and work requirements on those who get food stamps, much like those attached to welfare. Farm-state Republicans are distinctly unenthusiastic, though. And cutting spending on a program used by so many to put food on the table will never be popular.

SOCIAL SECURITY: PONZI SCHEME OR LIFESAVER?

Social Security, about one-fifth of all federal spending, is perhaps the most popular part of the federal budget. In polls, more than 80 percent of Americans say the seventy-five-year-old

The Social Security Problem

As the population ages, there will be fewer tax-paying workers for each Social Security beneficiary.

Workers per beneficiary

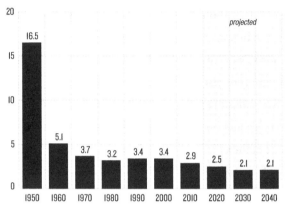

Source: Social Security Administration

program has been good for the country. Hardly anything else has such widespread support. In contrast to the recent close, partisan votes on major legislation, the original Social Security bill was passed in 1935 with substantial and bipartisan majorities in the House (272–33) and the Senate (77–6).

But Social Security is also one of the most misunderstood parts of the federal budget. "You cannot keep the status quo in place and call it anything other than a Ponzi scheme," Texas governor Rick Perry said in one Republican presidential debate in 2011. Underneath the harsh words was this point: the system depended on a large pool of younger workers to pay the benefits of those who joined the Social Security system in earlier years. Although many Americans believe that they are or will someday get back what they paid into Social Security, that's not how the program really works. Rather, today's payroll taxes go to pay benefits to today's retirees, whose benefits are linked by a complex formula to the wages they earned as workers. For a long time, there was more money coming in than going out, and this surplus was turned over to the Treasury. The Treasury spent the money and gave the famous Social Security Trust Fund IOUs, in the form of U.S. Treasury bonds, that essentially represent the commitments of future taxpayers to come up with the money needed to pay benefits.

That would have worked well if not for the baby boomers, the huge generation born between 1946 and 1964 that has begun to retire. The basic problem is actuarial: there won't be enough money coming into Social Security at current tax levels to pay benefits that have been promised, particularly once the baby boomers stop paying tax into the system and start claiming benefits. The number of taxpaying workers for every Social Security beneficiary has gone from 5.1 in 1960 to 2.9 today, and is projected to fall to 2.1 by 2029. In 2010, for the first time since the early 1980s, Social Security spent more in benefits than it collected in taxes, relying on the interest on its holdings of Treasury bonds to fill the gap. That math will hold for a while, but somewhere around 2036, the trust fund will be empty: if nothing is done before then, incoming tax revenues will cover only about 75 percent of the promised benefits.

Changes to Social Security are politically delicate because the program touches so many people. Nearly 55 million people, one out of every six Americans, were receiving Social Security benefits at the end of 2011, many more female than male because women live longer. Most who draw benefits are retired workers, but about 30 percent are disabled or are children, spouses, or, in a small number of cases, parents of workers who died. The average benefit for a retiree is $1,228.60 a month, or $14,750 a year. Those who had lower wages get less and those who had higher wages get more. Warren Buffett gets a Social Security check. But nearly half of Americans sixty-five or older would be below the poverty line if not for Social Security, and a quarter of the elderly get 90 percent of their income from the program.

One of them is Martha Soderberg, age seventy-three, who lives in Middlebury, Vermont, relying almost entirely on the $947.60 she gets each month from Social Security. Soderberg, widowed forty years ago and divorced from her second husband, worked about a decade as a nursery school teacher and then ran an inn with her second husband, who got the property in their divorce. She never thought much about saving for retirement, she says. She does own her house—the mortgage paid off with money she inherited from her mother—and has about $25,000 in mutual funds that her first husband left her. But other than that, her only income is the Social Security checks she has been getting since she turned sixty-two, and a little money she makes on the side selling handmade sweaters and doll clothes.

Soderberg isn't a complainer. "I feel like I'm getting by," she says. But that's only because of Social Security. What would she do without it? "One would presume that my two boys or my three sisters would keep me from going to the poorhouse," she answers. She obviously is no fan of cutting Social Security benefits for today's retirees–nor is anyone who proposes money-saving changes to Social Security talking about touching the already-retired–but she does read the newspaper headlines with more than a little frustration: "I do wish the government could do a better job of minding their accounts. We poor people have to."

HOW MANY AIRCRAFT CARRIERS IS ENOUGH?

By any yardstick, the Pentagon budget is huge. Last year's was equal to the value of all the goods and services produced in the economy of Indonesia, the fourth most populous country on Earth. The $700 billion total was 30 percent higher, adjusted for inflation, than the Cold War peak hit during Ronald Reagan's presidency. About $150 billon of that went for Iraq and Afghanistan, a sum that will wane as the troops come home. But even the rest of the defense budget–the peacetime budget known to insiders as "the base"–is higher than at any time since World War II. The central question now is how much the defense budget should be cut.

Leon Panetta was eager to cut the defense budget to reduce the deficit when he was chairman of the House Budget

The Defense Budget

The Pentagon's budget, adjusted for inflation, rose during the Iraq and Afghanistan wars to levels not seen since World War II. With those wars winding down, Obama's February 2012 budget proposed cutting the defense budget over the next few years, but he would leave spending higher than in previous periods of peace.

Billions of 2012 dollars

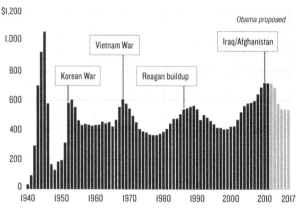

Source: White House Office of Management and Budget

Committee and White House budget director. As defense secretary, he's not quite as enthusiastic. To meet congressionally set spending caps, the Obama administration did propose a base defense budget for fiscal 2013 that is smaller than fiscal 2012's, the first such time it has done so, cutting $487 billion over ten years from its previous projections.

But Panetta was fiercely resisting an additional across-the-board cut that would be triggered in January 2013 if Congress and the president fail to agree on an alternative to reduce future deficits. "[A]fter 10 years of these cuts," Panetta wrote to Congress, "we would have the smallest ground force since 1940, the smallest number of ships since 1915 and the smallest Air Force in history." Skeptics were quick to note that the navy already has the fewest ships since 1916, that the types of ships now and then are quite different, that counting ships is hardly a measure of military might, that today's navy is larger than the next thirteen combined, and that across-the-board spending cuts would leave the Pentagon with as much money, adjusted for inflation, as it had in 2007, when there were few complaints about money for defense.

Panetta's cry is widely seen as a bargaining stance: the defense budget almost surely will be cut more in any deficit-reduction compromising, forcing the Pentagon to pare its long wish list. "We do not have and probably never will have enough money to buy all the things we could effectively use," military strategist Bernard Brodie said—in 1959. It's still true.

The bulk of the Pentagon's budget goes for three big items: personnel, operations and maintenance, and buying weapons. A close look at a couple of choices illuminates where the money goes, just how much this stuff costs, and why cutting the defense budget is so contentious.

Some of the decisions are too complex for ordinary civilians to understand. Others can be stated simply, such as: How many big aircraft carriers does the navy need to keep America safe? The price tag on these ships is staggering. The navy estimates each aircraft carrier costs in excess of $11 billion, more than Medicare spends annually on knee, hip, and shoulder joint replacements for nearly seven hundred thousand elderly. Aircraft carriers are expensive even in death: it costs about

$2 billion to decommission a carrier, including removing and storing two nuclear reactors.

The navy now has eleven big carriers, the oldest launched fifty years ago. The current plan is to replace one every five years with a new one–bigger, better, and much more expensive. The existing Nimitz class carriers are the largest warships in the world. The navy calls them "4.5 acres of mobile, sovereign U.S. territory." The new carriers will be about one-fifth of a mile long, capable of launching seventy-five aircraft from a flight deck almost as large as a football field. Partly because shipbuilding creates so many jobs and partly because aircraft carriers are such a symbol of military might, Congress, by law, requires the navy to maintain eleven carriers. It has, however, okayed a temporary plan to sail only ten carriers between the retirement of USS *Enterprise* in 2013 and the commissioning of the first of the new ones, USS *Gerald R. Ford*, in late 2015.

The more carriers, of course, the greater the navy's global reach and the greater the nation's capacity to send aircraft anywhere, even when no conveniently located nation is willing to offer a land base. The nagging question is this: Are aircraft carriers obsolete? Pearl Harbor, where so many U.S. planes were destroyed on the tarmac, demonstrated the strategic value of aircraft carriers, but that was sixty years ago. Today, the Chinese–now seen as the biggest potential maritime threat– are developing missiles that could render the modern carrier as vulnerable as the battleships at Pearl Harbor were.

"The need to project power across the oceans will never

go away," then defense secretary Robert Gates said in a 2010 speech. "But consider the massive over-match the U.S. already enjoys. Consider, too, the growing anti-ship capabilities of adversaries. Do we really need eleven carrier strike groups for another thirty years when no other country has more than one?" Some naval strategists suggest smaller, more flexible, amphibious ships carrying unmanned aircraft will be more valuable.

One money-saving option would be to retire an existing carrier ahead of time, reducing the carrier fleet to ten. Decommissioning rather than refueling the twenty-year-old USS *George Washington* in 2016 would save $7 billion over ten years, the CBO estimates, if the navy also cut its workforce by the 5,600 sailors who now man the ship. Obama reportedly rejected this option during internal budget negotiations. "The president feels strongly that, if we're going to have a presence in the Pacific, cutting a carrier would undercut the message," Panetta said, adding that savings elsewhere in the navy budget made room for the carrier. But when Congress eyes further cuts in the defense budget, as it is likely to do at some point, the need for an eleventh carrier will be reexamined.

The Pentagon is more than an armada, though. It's also among the world's largest employers, with all that implies. In May 2010, Gates marked the sixty-fifth anniversary of the Allied victory in Europe with a speech at the Dwight D. Eisenhower Presidential Library in Abilene, Kansas. He spoke not about General Eisenhower's battlefield victories but about President Eisenhower's frustrations with the defense budget, which Gates clearly shared. Some of their concerns were similar. Both were frustrated at the military's insatiable appetite for new weapons. Some of their concerns were different. Eisenhower complained that it took the army fifty years to get rid of horses. Gates complained, "Health care costs are eating the Defense Department alive." Eisenhower would have been stunned.

When Gates spoke, the Defense Department was spending as much on health care–about $50 billion–as on the war in Iraq. The tab has risen since; in 2011 it came to $54 billion. Health care consumes about 10 percent of the defense budget (excluding the costs of Iraq and Afghanistan). One big reason: Tricare, the military health insurance program created in 1995, is significantly more generous than insurance offered to other employees. Yet, every attempt by the White House or Pentagon to curb the benefits, Gates said, "meets with a furious response from the Congress and veterans groups. The proposals routinely die an ignominious death on Capitol Hill"–even though none of the changes would affect active-duty military or wounded warriors in the care of the Veterans Administration's health system.

Why does Tricare survive unscathed? Mostly because of the enormous political power of veterans' groups. "They've always been very strong, and when you've been in ten years of war, the veterans get that much more leverage," Panetta said recently. The rising cost of wages, health insurance, and retirement–"if it keeps growing on the path that it's on now"–

will "eat away at our ability to provide the training, the equipment, and all the other things that are basic to our defense," he said.

Few outsiders appreciate how generous Tricare is. About 15 percent of enlisted men and women and 50 percent of officers stay in the military the twenty years needed to qualify for health insurance after they "retire," often in their forties. The annual premium was set at $460 a year per family in 1995, and for those who signed up before October 1, 2011, it hasn't changed since. For personnel who enrolled after that, the premium has been boosted–to a still-bargain price of $520. For similar coverage, federal civilian workers pay around $5,000 a year. "Try to change . . . that, and you get 'You're not a patriot,' " says Alan Simpson, the retired Republican senator who cochaired a deficit-reduction panel with Erskine Bowles. Obama's latest budget, though, proposes significant premium increases over the next five years, bigger ones for those with bigger pensions.

The health plan is so generous that most of those who retire from the military and take other jobs turn down their new employers' insurance because Tricare is a much better deal. Among them is Francis Brady, a retired marine lieutenant colonel in his early fifties who was earning six figures at the consulting firm Booz Allen when he was interviewed by the *New York Times* in 2010. Tricare, he said, is "so cheap compared to what Booz Allen has. . . . [It's] phenomenal." So it's no surprise that a growing share of military retirees and their families are signing up for the government coverage instead of the insurance offered by their new employers.

Later, when military retirees reach age sixty-five and become eligible for Medicare, a program called Tricare for Life picks up the tab for insurance to cover things that Medicare doesn't. Other Americans pay around $2,100 a year for such policies. Tricare for Life "is costing us $11 billion a year in the defense budget . . . basically enough to buy a new [aircraft] carrier every year," says Todd Harrison, a budget analyst at the Center for Strategic and Budgetary Assessments, a defense think tank.

FROM DIRT DAM SAFETY TO LANDING ON MARS

Much of what Americans think of as "the government" is the remaining 18 percent of federal spending that Congress appropriates annually for a hodgepodge of domestic programs. This money, $566 billion last year, goes for salaries of everyone from the president to the cooks in federal prisons. It aids inner-city schools in Chicago, subsidizes housing for the poor in Omaha, inspects meatpacking plants in Chino, California, and operates air-traffic control towers outside Atlanta. Most of what can be considered an investment in future productivity or economic growth falls in this bucket: bridges, broadband networks, research at the National Institutes of Health, prekindergarten classes for poor kids, and on and on. This is called "non-defense *discretionary* spending" because it's subject to annual congressional votes, unlike "mandatory" Social Security or Medicare benefits. In recent years, it has been swollen by Obama's fiscal stimulus. Last year, Congress passed a law that sets spending for the next ten years, yet another attempt to tie its hands and keep increases on these expenditures below the rate of inflation over time. While it's easy to argue that somewhere in this half trillion dollars a year are examples of government excess, this new austerity inevitably will limit funding for programs valued by someone, no matter if they have huge profiles and big budgets (the National Aeronautics and Space Administration) or are virtually unknown (the National Dam Safety Program).

The United States' biggest dams—among them, Hoover on the Nevada/Arizona border, Oroville in California, and Mossyrock in Washington State—are owned by the federal government or by big government-run utilities. But 65 percent of dams in the United States are privately owned, nearly all of them small earthen structures built years ago; most of the rest are owned by state and local governments. With all the demands on the federal budget, the safety of these lesser dams might be seen as one thing Washington could leave to the states, and indeed every state but one (Alabama) has a law regulating dam safety. But according to the American Society of Civil Engineers, "Many state dam safety programs do not have sufficient resources, funding, or staff to conduct dam safety inspections, to take appropriate enforcement actions, or to ensure proper construction by reviewing plans and performing construction inspections." South Dakota, for example, has only three dam inspectors–one for every 782 dams. In Iowa, it's one for every 1,674 dams. When these dams do fail, the results can be devastating.

A 1972 dam collapse in West Virginia claimed 125 lives. Another–in Idaho, in 1976–resulted in eleven deaths. The following year, thirty-nine people died when a dam failed in Jimmy Carter's home state of Georgia, prompting the new president and Congress to step in to protect people and property downstream. The Army Corps of Engineers was told to build what's now the National Inventory of Dams (84,134 at last count, 17 percent of them deemed very hazardous). And thus was born the National Dam Safety Program, eventually reorganized into the Federal Emergency Management Agency, which now lives within the sprawling Department of Homeland Security.

The program–which officially coordinates the Interagency Committee on Dam Safety–employs just three people and operated last year with a budget of only $8.9 million. Most of that gets spread around the states to pay for inspectors who check the dams and are supposed to get owners to prepare emergency evacuation plans and fix dangerous conditions. In budgeting, the more an office spends, the more advocates it has, which ought to make the minuscule National Dam Safety Program ripe for plucking. But it has a protective political edge: no one wants to argue that the country would be better off letting unsafe dams deteriorate further. Besides, protecting the nation's infrastructure–including bridges, dams, and levees–became sacrosanct after 9/11. And so the National Dam Safety Program, like hundreds of similar federal backwaters, soldiers on. In the early 1990s, Susan Tanaka, who is now research director at the Peter G. Peterson Foundation, says she tried to kill the program when she worked at the Office of Management and Budget. "Most of the dams are on private property and pose no threat to public safety," she reasoned. "The program is too small to do much and it didn't seem a national priority." She failed. "It was too small for anyone to care about," she says today. All those "too smalls" add up, though.

TO THE MOON, BUT NOT TO MARS?

NASA is as famous as the National Dam Safety Program is obscure, and a heck of a lot bigger. Created in 1958 to explore space separately from the military, the agency was not yet three years old when it was asked by John F. Kennedy to put a man on the moon before the end of the decade–and it did. At its peak in the mid-1960s, NASA accounted for more than 4 percent of all federal spending. Today, the agency spends, adjusted for inflation, about half what it did then and its budget represents about 0.5 percent of all federal spending. It's still a substantial sum: $18.5 billion last year, roughly the size of the entire budget of the state of Iowa.

Polls suggest the public remains enthusiastic about spending money to explore space. A 2011 Pew Research Center poll found 58 percent deemed it "essential" for the United States "to continue to be a world leader in space exploration." In a Gallup poll taken on the fortieth anniversary of the 1969 moon landing, an identical 58 percent said the space program has brought enough benefits to justify its costs. Presidents of both parties and many members of Congress offer lofty rhetoric about it. In 2004, George W. Bush directed NASA to focus on returning humans to the moon by 2020, and then sending them to Mars and "worlds beyond." Before the end of the decade, though, it became clear that fulfilling these missions would cost far more than either the White House or Congress was prepared to spend. Obama scrapped the return trip to the moon but promised to come up with enough money so humans could orbit Mars by 2030 and land there in his lifetime. "Space exploration is not a luxury," he said in a speech at the Kennedy Space Center in Florida. "It's not an afterthought in America's quest for a brighter future—it is an essential part of that quest."

In that speech, delivered on Tax Day, April 15, 2010, Obama raised the pregnant question for a debt-burdened government: "Why spend money on NASA at all? Why spend money solving problems in space when we don't lack for problems to solve here on the ground? We have massive structural deficits that have to be closed in the coming years." But that is "a false choice," he insisted. "For pennies on the dollar, the space program has improved our lives, advanced our society, strengthened our economy, and inspired generations of Americans." Not to mention creating jobs. NASA administrator Charles Bolden noted as he unveiled the agency's budget in 2012: "Every dollar spent on space exploration is spent here on Earth."

Still, Congress has been squeezing NASA's budget–by $250 million in 2011, or 1.2 percent less than the year before. For 2012, Congress pared another $685 million, or 3.7 percent. And in February 2012, Obama proposed shaving $59 million from NASA's overall budget in fiscal year 2013 to make room for other spending under the congressionally imposed cap. That still left room for, among other things, the 2018 launch of the increasingly expensive James Webb Space Telescope, with its mirror twenty-one feet in diameter and a sun shield as large as a tennis court; education and administration (more than $600 million a year); and the U.S. share of the International Space Station ($3 billion a year).

But Obama's "false choice," it turned out, was a real one. Over objections from some at NASA, the White House proposed a 20 percent–$300 million–cut in the budget for planetary science, ending U.S. participation in a European venture to send an unmanned explorer to Mars. That prompted the resignation of the head of NASA's science mission, Ed Weiler. "The Mars program is one of the crown jewels of NASA," Weiler says. "In what irrational, Homer Simpson world would we single it out for cuts?"

NASA administrator Bolden's explanation: "We could not afford the path we were on." He insisted, though, that the United States remains intent on exploring Mars.

Nearly all of the belt-tightening in the federal budget in the past year and a half has been focused on these last two pieces of the pie, defense and annually appropriated domestic programs. But that won't be nearly enough to bring the deficit and national debt down to sustainable levels; hence the focus on Medicare, Medicaid, and Social Security–and on taxes, the subject of the next chapter.

CHAPTER 4

WHERE THE MONEY COMES FROM

Taxing the people to raise money for the government has ancient roots. In Genesis, Joseph decreed that one-fifth of every farmer's crop should go to Pharaoh. Large parts of the Rosetta Stone, carved around 200 B.C., detail a tax exemption for priests. In the seventeenth century, Britain's Charles I relied on "forced loans" from landowners, who weren't repaid. In the eighteenth century, England and Scotland taxed windows; the rich had more of them than the poor. Peter the Great taxed beards in czarist Russia. In 1799, Britain, no longer collecting taxes from its former colonies in America, imposed an income tax to finance a war against France.

Today the U.S. federal government gets money primarily in two ways: it taxes and it borrows—a lot of each. Last year, it collected $2.3 trillion in taxes, fees, and other revenues—about $19,400 per household—and borrowed another $1.1 trillion, or $9,300 per household, committing future generations to tax themselves to pay that back.

Today, most federal tax revenues come from the income

tax on individuals (47 percent last year) and the payroll tax on employers and employees (36 percent).

It wasn't always this way.

Until the Civil War, the U.S. government relied almost exclusively on tariffs on imported goods, a practice that provoked conflict between Northern manufacturers who favored tariffs to keep imports out and Southern farmers who did not. An income tax was imposed during the Civil War, but proved so unpopular that it died in 1872. In its place, the government imposed taxes on alcohol and tobacco that accounted for 43 percent of all federal revenue by 1900. Repeated attempts to revive the income tax were thwarted when the Supreme Court declared it unconstitutional in 1895. But the Sixteenth Amendment to the Constitution changed that. Less than eight months after it was ratified in February 1913, Congress enacted an income tax. It was this new source of tax revenue that made Prohibition possible six years later. "After the income tax was passed, reformers realized there was a replacement for the revenue that came from taxing alcohol, and they started to push for a constitutional amendment," according to Daniel Okrent, author of a history of Prohibition.

Initially, the income tax hit only the rich, those with incomes above $20,000, the equivalent of $450,000 in today's dollars. The top marginal tax rate, the slice of each additional dollar of income the government took from the very best off, was 7 percent on earnings over $500,000, equivalent to $11 million today. The need for money to fight World War II democratized the income tax. "Because of the need for a lot of revenue fast, personal income taxation was expanded dramatically during World War II ... transforming what had been a 'class tax' into a 'mass tax,'" economists Joel Slemrod and Jon Bakija wrote in *Taxing Ourselves: A Citizen's Guide to the Great Debate over Tax Reform.*

In the years since, tax rates have risen and fallen in intervening years almost as much as hemlines. The top marginal rate hit an astounding 92 percent in the 1950s, though few actually paid that because there were so many ways to avoid it and so much reason to do so. Ronald Reagan's landmark Tax Reform Act of 1986 brought it down to 28 percent by eliminating deductions, exemptions, and tax shelters, which is known as broadening the tax base. Today's top marginal rate, 35 percent, applies to couples with taxable income (that is, after deductions and credits) of $338,350 and up. Obama wants to raise the rate; Republicans want to lower it.

The payroll tax–levied on wages but not capital gains, interest, or dividends–was imposed in 1937 to finance Social Security. It was expanded in 1965 to help fund Medicare and enlarged in 1983 to shore up Social Security. Before Medicare was born, the payroll tax accounted for only about one-sixth of all federal revenue. Today, it accounts for more than one-third.

In contrast, the tax on corporate profits, born in 1909, is a shrinking share of federal revenue. In the early 1950s, more than 30 percent of federal revenues came from the corporate income tax. Last year, revenues accounted for an unusually

The Changing Tax Mix

The individual income tax is a mainstay for the federal government.
Payroll taxes have grown in importance, while corporate income taxes
have shrunk.

Percentage of GDP

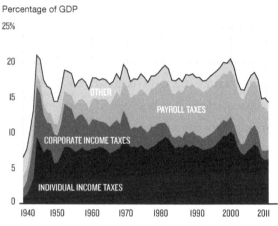

Source: White House Office of Management and Budget

low 7.9 percent, but as the economy returns to normal, it is
projected under the current tax code to account for about 12
percent of federal revenues over the next few years.

Why such a declining share? In part, because Congress
has offered corporations all sorts of tax breaks. And, in part,
because businesses have exploited loopholes or shifted profits overseas or legally organized themselves into entities that
aren't subject to the corporate tax. (That last factor is a big one:
in 1980, 22 percent of all U.S. business profits were booked by
outfits organized so they didn't pay corporate taxes, though
their owners–like partners in a law firm–paid individual in-

come taxes on the profits. In 2008, 73 percent of all business profits were in entities that didn't pay corporate taxes.)

With competition from abroad to attract businesses increasingly stiff, most economists and many politicians challenge the wisdom of relying more heavily on corporate taxes. Both the White House and congressional Republicans were flirting with corporate tax reform in early 2012, but both were talking about rearranging the burden among businesses, not raising more money from corporations.

The federal government's only explicit tax on wealth–the estate tax levied on the money that the wealthy leave when they die–was an important source of revenue in the 1930s but has been on the wane ever since. Last year, it accounted for much less than 1 percent of revenues. Unlike most other developed countries, the United States at the federal level doesn't rely on broad sales taxes on consumer spending, such as the value-added tax common abroad.

This book focuses on the federal government, but Americans pay state and local taxes, too. For every $1 the federal government raised in 2011, state and local governments collected another 58 cents from sales, property, income, and other taxes. That measure recently has been distorted by the federal government's ability to cut taxes and run deficits during a recession; most states can't do that. But even before the recession, the weight of state and local taxes rose from 44 cents for every $1 of federal taxes in 2001 to 49 cents in 2007. Of course,

DAVID WESSEL

the burden varies widely by state. State and local governments in New York take about 15 percent of personal income, while in Missouri they take about 9 percent.

WHO MAKES THESE DAMN TAX LAWS ANYHOW?

Details of tax laws—more than almost anything else Congress does—are largely the province of congressional and Treasury staff tax experts and battalions of well-paid lobbyists. Particularly the lobbyists. At last count, more than 12,500 people were registered as lobbyists in Washington, all trying to influence the government, many of them toiling over an obscure piece of the tax code that matters to a handful of companies.

Among them is Jon Talisman. He is a balding tax lawyer and accountant who would never be cast as a flashy lobbyist in a Hollywood drama about money and politics. But he is both typical and highly successful, regularly named one of the two or three dozen most influential lobbyists in Washington. Talisman spent eight years as a tax lawyer in private practice, six as a congressional staffer, and another four years as a top tax official in the Treasury during the Clinton administration, much of that time waging war against tax shelters. In 2000, he turned to lobbying because, he says, "Gore lost and I got fired."

He formed Capitol Tax Partners, a firm that, like most oth-

108

ers, deliberately mixes tax experts who once worked for Democrats with others who had worked for Republicans. The firm's client list includes brand-name companies like Delta Airlines, Federal Express, JPMorgan Chase, Time Warner, and 3M that pay retainers of between $10,000 and $20,000 a month. Talisman's office in a modern building at 101 Constitution Avenue is triangular in shape. The placement of the conference table in front of a large window tells clients they've come to the right place: Talisman sits with his back to the window. The client sits on the other side. Over Talisman's shoulder, perfectly framed in the window, is the U.S. Capitol building.

The job of getting or protecting tax breaks for companies is harder than it used to be, Talisman says. One reason is the overwhelming size of looming federal budget deficits. "Everybody understands that deficits make everything in the tax arena harder," he says. "Tax reform"–the always popular, always politically treacherous goal of making the tax code simpler and smarter–"is really difficult when you can't throw money at it. Losers always squeak louder than winners cheer," he says. Another reason is the passing of the day when there was bipartisan cooperation to fix glaring problems in the tax code–outdated provisions, conflicting requirements, abused loopholes, sections that had been challenged by the courts. "You didn't worry about whether it raised revenue or lost revenue," he recalled. "Today, if it raises revenue, it's a tax increase. And if it loses revenue, it's a special-interest provision." And either one makes it controversial.

RESISTING TAXES: FROM LADY GODIVA
TO GROVER NORQUIST

Taxes are never popular, and resistance is perennial, sometimes successful. According to eleventh-century legend, Lady
Godiva repeatedly begged her husband, Leofric, to lift heavy
taxes he had imposed on the people of Coventry. He relented
on one condition: that she ride naked on horseback through
the streets. After demanding that everyone stay inside behind
closed windows and doors, Godiva took her famous ride, and
Leofric kept his promise. (A fellow named Tom, the story goes,
cut a hole in his shutters to watch her–the original "Peeping
Tom.") The Boston Tea Party of 1773 was a reaction to the
British tax on imported tea. The American Revolution was
fought, in part, over colonists' anger at "taxation without rep-
resentation." In 1794, in what was known as the Whiskey Rebellion, Pennsylvania farmers attacked federal agents trying to
collect a tax on whiskey. The insurrection was forcibly quashed
by George Washington, but populist anger at taxes has been a
recurring theme in American politics ever since.

In today's Washington, one cannot talk about taxes without mentioning Grover Norquist, a round-faced Harvard MBA
with a closely cropped beard who has been a Republican activist since he volunteered for Nixon's 1968 campaign at age
twelve. Norquist, fifty-five, has had a single mission since Ronald Reagan recruited him from the staff of the U.S. Chamber
of Commerce in 1985 to build an organization to push for tax

reform–i.e., to fight increases in tax rates. Nearly thirty years ago, Norquist's Americans for Tax Reform asked members of Congress to sign "the pledge" that they'll oppose any tax increases. "It's very difficult to lie when you write it down," Norquist says.

Norquist has helped brand the Republican Party as the antitax party. Republicans who violate his pledge, he says, are as damaging to the image as reports of rat heads in Coke bottles would be to the Coca-Cola brand, he says. His organization raised more than $13 million in 2010, according to its latest available IRS filings.

Norquist is not subtle. He keeps a miniature bathtub on his desk, a reference to a 2001 NPR interview in which he famously declared: "I don't want to abolish government. I simply want to reduce it to the size where I can drag it into the bathroom and drown it in the bathtub." He is funny, though, the runner-up in a Washington's funniest celebrity contest. (A sample: "I'm drinking bourbon neat. No water. I never drink water. Dick Cheney tortures with it." Another, coming from the father of two: "The person who came up with the phrase 'sleeps like a baby' was an eighth-century eunuch who had never seen a baby, and had certainly never seen one try to sleep.")

Norquist insists the no-tax-increases pledge is made to voters, not to him, but he has become the arbiter of what policies would or wouldn't violate the promise. That has made him a huge obstacle for those of both parties who see no way to bring the deficit under control except by raising taxes *and*

cutting spending. Among them is Tom Coburn, a fiercely independent, conservative Republican senator from Oklahoma
who began as a manager in the family manufacturing business,
then went to medical school and became a family doctor and
obstetrician. After six years in the House, Coburn left in 2001,
keeping a vow to serve no more than three terms. But he came
back to Congress as a senator four years later and lately has
been among a bipartisan band—dubbed the Gang of Six—trying
to fashion a package of tax increases and spending cuts to reduce the deficit. When he successfully pushed to eliminate a
tax break for ethanol, Norquist accused him of having "lied
his way into office" because the resulting increase in revenues
wasn't used to reduce other taxes. "Which pledge is most important," Coburn asked on *Meet the Press*, "the pledge to uphold
your oath to the Constitution of the United States or a pledge
from a special interest group who claims to speak for all of
American conservatives when in fact they really don't?"

WHO PAYS? HOW MUCH?

In the high-volume debate over taxes, facts about basic issues—
who pays? how much? who doesn't?—often get lost, twisted, or
distorted. Perhaps the most salient and overlooked fact is this
one: *for most Americans, federal taxes have not risen over the past
couple of decades.*

Over the last thirty years, the U.S. tax collector has sliced

The Tax Bite

The share of income paid in federal taxes of all kinds by Americans at the bottom and in the middle of the income distribution has fallen steadily over the past thirty years. For those in the top fifth and for the now-famous 1 percent, the average tax rate has bounced around, but is lower today than it was thirty years ago.

Average tax rate

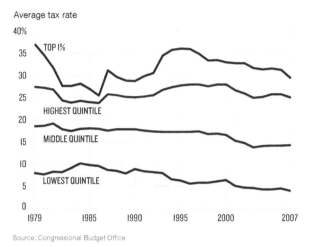

Source: Congressional Budget Office

for itself a share of the national economic pie of about 18 percent of the GDP, which is the broadest way to measure the tax burden. The government's take hit 19.6 percent in 1981 as Ronald Reagan was arriving in Washington, fell in subsequent years due to tax-cutting and recessions, and peaked at 20.6 percent in 2006 as George W. Bush was running for president, which was one of the forces that drove his tax-cut proposals. Before the Great Recession arrived in 2007, taxes as a share of GDP were hovering around 18.5 percent. Lately, the tax take has been unusually low–15.4 percent of GDP last year. That's the consequence of the very weak economy and tax cuts

The Rich Make More and Pay More

The best-paid Americans get a far bigger slice of the national income than those at the bottom, and they pay more taxes. The bottom fifth got 3.7% of all the income in 2011 and paid only 0.2% of all federal taxes. The 1 percent, in contrast, got 16.8% of the income and paid 25.6% of the taxes.

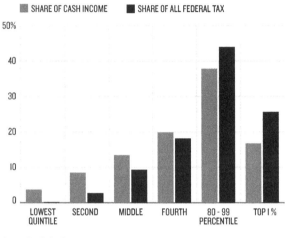

Source: Tax Policy Center

enacted in response. The CBO projects that if current policies persist–that is, even if all the Bush tax cuts are renewed beyond December 31, 2012–revenues will rise gradually, returning to the 18 percent of GDP average in 2017.

For ordinary Americans, the tax take as a percentage of GDP is hard to comprehend. Their question is simpler: how much of my paycheck does the government take? That answer depends on how much money they make and whether their income derives from wages or more lightly taxed profits from trading stocks or other capital gains.

Although many taxpaying Americans suspect otherwise,

the share of the income that most of them have been paying to Washington has been coming down over the past few decades.

Consider taxpayers on the middle rungs of the ladder: the 60 percent of households whose incomes put them neither in the top fifth nor the bottom fifth–the ones with incomes these days between $16,800 and $103,500 a year. Their federal *income* taxes fell, on average, from about 8 percent of their income in 1979 to around 4 percent in 2007, according to the latest CBO estimates.

Then add the payroll tax, generally split between employer and employee, which has been taking a bigger and bigger bite. The payroll tax is a big deal. In 2011, about 40 percent of all households paid more in the *employee* share of the payroll tax than they paid in federal income taxes. Combining the *employee* and *employer* shares of taxes (because the employer share comes out of the wages they would otherwise pay and because the self-employed pay both halves themselves), over 60 percent of households paid more in payroll than income taxes.

The payroll tax rate has more than doubled over the past fifty years, and the ceiling on the wages to which it applies has risen with inflation. But because wages for the best-paid workers have been rising faster than those of other workers, the tax hit a shrinking fraction of all wages paid in the economy. The current tax rate is 15.3 percent–12.4 percent for Social Security (on wages up to $110,100 in 2012) and another 2.9 percent for Medicare (without any wage ceiling). At Obama's urging, Congress has for the past couple of years declared a temporary 2-percentage-point tax holiday for workers. That is likely to disappear as the economy recovers. Beginning in 2013, Obama's health reform law, the Affordable Care Act, imposes an additional 0.9% Medicare payroll tax on wages over $200,000 for individuals and over $250,000 for couples, and adds a new 3.8 percent tax on their investment income.

A full tax accounting has to include not only income and payroll taxes, but taxes imposed on corporations that eventually are passed along to consumers, workers, and shareholders. Add them in and, by the CBO's reckoning, that middle 60 percent of taxpayers paid about 19 percent of their income in federal taxes of all kinds, direct and indirect, in 1979. In 2007, it was down to 15 percent. In 2011, according to separate estimates by the Tax Policy Center, it was down to 13 percent.

No one enjoys paying taxes, but public opinion polls suggest the attitude toward taxes is more complex than the rhetoric of antitax politicians sometimes suggests. In fact, recent surveys find fewer Americans complaining about the size of their federal tax bill. In December 2011, for instance, the Pew Research Center asked: "Considering what you get from the federal government, do you think you pay more than your fair share of taxes, less than your fair share or about the right amount?" Some 52 percent answered "the right amount," significantly more than the 41 percent who gave the same answer in March 2003 shortly after Bush cut taxes significantly. Pew's polls are no fluke. Gallup's shows a similar trend.

For a lot of Americans, the issue isn't the size of their tax bill, but whether the tax code is—in their minds—"fair." As Pew puts it, "The focus of the public's frustration is not how much they themselves pay, but rather the impression that wealthy people are not paying their fair share." In the December 2011 Pew poll, 55 percent said the U.S. tax system isn't fair.

TAX RETURNS: FROM NIXON TO ROMNEY

This off-again, on-again "fairness" issue surfaced early in the 2012 Republican presidential primaries when Mitt Romney, reluctantly, released his 104-page tax return. "Tax returns of the rich and famous have a way of highlighting important policy issues that often get ignored in public debate," tax columnist Joseph J. Thorndike said at the time. Indeed.

Romney's return revealed that he and his wife had income of $20.9 million in 2011 and paid $3.2 million in federal income and payroll taxes. In other words, they paid about 15 percent of their gross take (that is, before deductions) in federal income and payroll taxes, much less than the typical upper-income taxpayer. Romney's income was largely from capital gains (taxed at a lower rate than wages), and his taxes were reduced by big deductible charitable contributions, mainly to the Mormon Church.

The controversy over Romney's taxes was nothing compared to the one that erupted over Richard Nixon's during the Watergate scandal. On November 17, 1973, four hundred newspaper editors gathered at Walt Disney World for a televised question-and-answer session with the president. Nixon was tense. He had been reelected, but his presidency was on the rocks. He joked that if Air Force One went down, Congress "wouldn't have to impeach." The joke drew laughs, but the editors pressed him about the Watergate break-in and subsequent cover-up as well as a less-remembered scandal: his taxes.

The *Wall Street Journal* had reported that the president's handwritten tax returns (fewer than twenty pages each) revealed that he had paid just $5,100 in combined federal income taxes for 1970, 1971, and 1972 on income that totaled $795,000. His 1970 tax bill was only $792. It would have been zero if not for the alternative minimum tax enacted in 1969 over Nixon's objections, to make sure no one got so many deductions and credits that he or she came close to avoiding taxes altogether. The new tax followed testimony by the Treasury secretary that 155 households with incomes above $200,000 in 1967 (about $1.4 million in today's dollars) hadn't paid any income taxes. Tax historians speculate that Nixon's $792 bill in 1970 may have been made him the first AMT taxpayer.

It was during questioning about all this that Nixon uttered the famous words: "I'm not a crook. I've earned everything I've got." That was true, but he had cheated on his taxes. He took a questionable $576,000 deduction for donating his vice presidential papers to the government, though the transfer documents were later found to have been backdated. He overdid the home-office deductions for his San Clemente, California, house, claiming it was his primary residence even though he was living in the White House, and then, to top matters off, he didn't pay state taxes in California despite alleging that he was living there. After audits by the IRS and, because the Nixon White House had so undermined the credibility of the IRS, audits by the staff of the congressional Joint Committee on Taxation, Nixon ultimately agreed to pay $465,000 in back taxes for those years. No surprise, every president since Nixon has released his tax returns voluntarily. Nixon's successor, Gerald Ford, reported paying more than $95,000 in federal income taxes in 1975 on gross income of $252,000, a 38 percent tax rate.

The flap over Nixon's taxes, largely forgotten today, focused public attention at the time on the "fairness" of the tax code—who should be asked to pay how much—and the capacity of the best off to find ways to reduce their taxes. That debate has been revived lately for reasons beyond Romney's tax returns: the gap between winners and losers in the U.S. economy has been widening substantially. Underlying the debate over how much to tax the rich is a fundamental disagreement about how hard the government should use the tax code to resist that tendency. Obama would raise taxes on those with incomes above $250,000: "Those who have done well, including me, should pay our fair share in taxes to contribute to the nation that made our success possible," he argued. Romney objected. His counterargument: "You know, there was a time in this country that we didn't celebrate attacking people based on their success and when we didn't go after people because they were successful."

It is important to understand the starting point. Today's tax code does take more from the rich than from the middle class and the poor. The political issues are whether the rich, whose share of national income has been growing, should pay even more and whether making them do so would have undesirable side effects on the economy. Here's where things stand today, based on estimates covering all federal taxes–income, payroll, and corporate–produced by the Tax Policy Center:

- The bottom 40 percent of Americans, whose gross incomes were below $33,500, got 12 percent of the income in 2011 and paid 3 percent of all federal taxes.

- The middle class, the 40 percent of Americans with incomes between $33,500 and $103,000, got 33 percent of the income and paid 27 percent of the taxes

- The best-off 20 percent, whose incomes range upward from $103,000, got 55 percent of the income and paid 70 percent of the taxes.

That last group includes some really well-off people, of course. Zooming in on them, the Tax Policy Center estimates:

- Those famously branded "the 1%" by the Occupy Wall Street protesters, the ones with incomes above $533,000 in 2011, got 17 percent of the income and paid 26 percent of the taxes.

- The top-top tier, the 0.1%, the 120,000 taxpayers with incomes above $2.2 million—think Goldman Sachs partners, Microsoft's Bill Gates, the megastars of sports and music—got 8 percent of all the income in 2011 (which, by the way, is four times the size of the slice the top 0.1% got thirty years earlier). They paid 13 percent of all federal taxes.

And then there are the Fortunate Four Hundred. For years, Congress has required the IRS to report each year on the income taxes paid by the four hundred taxpayers with the highest incomes without identifying them. The snapshot for 2008, the latest available, is illuminating. To make the list, one had to have income in that one year of $110 million; the average for the group was above $270 million, down from the boom year of 2007 but more than comfortable. The ranks of the Fortunate Four Hundred aren't stable: people move in and out; about one hundred of them have made the list more than once in the seventeen years for which the IRS reports the data.

As a group, these four hundred taxpayers paid 18.1 percent of their gross income in taxes. "The very rich not only made lots more money, they made it in a very different way," Roberton Williams of the Tax Policy Center observed. Nearly 60 percent of their gross income in 2008 came from capital gains, nearly all of it taxed at a 15 percent rate. Only 8 percent of their income came from wages taxed at a marginal rate of 35 percent. In contrast, the rest of the population got only

5 percent of its income from capital gains and 72 percent from wages.

Over the years, under both Republican and Democratic presidents, the tax burden on those at the bottom of the pyramid has been steadily lightened. One big reason is the earned income tax credit, created by Senator Russell Long, the Louisiana Democrat who, in 1975, was seeking an alternative to spending more on welfare. The EITC is a bonus the government pays the working poor, reducing the taxes they would otherwise owe or, depending on their circumstances, giving them cash. After food stamps, the EITC is now the federal government's biggest antipoverty program, worth nearly $60 billion in 2011 to 27 million households, more than one in every five households.

"SPENDING THROUGH THE TAX CODE"

For ordinary Americans, there's the money you take in and the money you spend. The federal budget doesn't work that way. No discussion of taxes can avoid the money that the government doesn't collect because of some provision of the tax code, a deduction or a credit or an exclusion or an exemption. In response to years of calls to control "spending" and "smaller government," Congress and presidents have discovered something simple: giving people a tax break—a credit, a loophole, a deduction—makes them happy without increasing government "spending" and can accomplish the same objective. Practically and economically, there's no difference between getting $1,000 in cash from the government and getting a $1,000 voucher that you can use to reduce your taxes. Either results in a federal budget deficit that's $1,000 bigger than it would have been had the tax break not been created. But the first is called "spending" (boos, hisses) and the second is called "a tax cut" (applause, cheers). The first is formally recorded on the budget books as an outflow of money. The second doesn't show up in the outflow and inflow accounting. It is revenue that wasn't collected. By the same logic, the Earned Income Tax Credit is a way for the government to spend money–in this case, giving money to low-wage workers–without counting it as spending.

The late tax economist David Bradford once joked that Congress could wipe out the defense budget and replace it with a Weapons Supply Tax Credit. Arms makers, he said, would be allowed to save enough money on taxes to cover whatever the government would have paid them. Then the government would announce that through "targeted tax relief," taxes had been slashed without jeopardizing national security or increasing the deficit. But nothing would have changed: the same labor, energy, and materials would have been taken by the government to make the weapons.

It's no longer a joke.

These "tax expenditures," as they're called in Washington patois, add up to a lot of money. There's a credit for adopting a child, another for investing in biomass generation of electricity, and the popular deduction for home-mortgage interest. More than 60 percent of all federal subsidies for energy are routed through the tax system rather than through direct spending. Put all these together, and they added up to $1.1 trillion in forgone revenue in 2011, the Treasury calculates. That's enormous, given that the total revenues of the U.S. government that year were $2.3 trillion.

Erskine Bowles calls them "backdoor spending through the tax code." He told (yet another) congressional deficit-reduction committee last year, "It is just spending by another name. It's somebody's social policy." The deficit-reduction commission he cochaired recommended doing away with most of them, and using the money to lower tax rates and reduce the deficit.

The Tax Reform Act of 1986 stripped away many barnacles from the tax code, wiping out tax shelters, raising taxes on businesses, and using the money to lower individual income tax rates. The barnacles grew back, though. Today, about 10 percent of the spending through tax-code savings goes to businesses and 90 percent to individuals, notably the provisions that allow workers to get health insurance from employers without paying taxes on that as wages ($184.5 billion in 2012) and homeowners to deduct mortgage interest ($98.6 billion). If all the tax expenditures in the *corporate* tax code were wiped out, which will never happen, the tax rate on big companies could fall from 35 percent to 28 percent and raise the same amount of money.

The saga of a tax break known as Section 1031 for its place in the tax code shows how entrenched these are. If you sell a share of Microsoft stock at a profit, you owe capital gains taxes even if you immediately put the proceeds into shares of Google. But if you swap one office building for another, and play by 1031 rules, that's considered "a like-kind exchange," and you can defer—or, if you're clever, avoid—capital gains taxes. "All real estate, in particular, is considered 'like-kind,' allowing a retiring farmer from the Midwest to swap farm land for a Florida apartment building or a right to pump water tax-free," the Congressional Research Service has said. The revenues lost through this one provision were about $2.5 billion in 2011. It's relatively small, but illustrative.

Like so many tax breaks, this one began long ago for reasons that have little to do with its current size. It popped up in 1921 when the income tax was in its youth, to allow investors to avoid taxes when swapping property without a "readily realizable market value." In 1934, the tax-writing House Ways and Means Committee explained, "If all exchanges were to be made taxable, it would be necessary to evaluate the property received in exchange in thousands of horse trades." Over the years, it has been tweaked and the definition of "like-kind" shrunk, stretched, and reinterpreted.

Today, one can swap a dental office for a vacation property and avoid taxes, if you structure the deal the right way. One can trade horses, cattle, hogs, mules, donkeys, sheep, goats, and other animals owned for investment, breeding, or sporting, advises Andy Gustafson, a 1031 broker, but not chickens, turkeys, pigeons, fish, frogs, or reptiles. But you can't trade a bull for a milk cow and avoid taxes: "Livestock of different sexes," the IRS cautions, "are not like-kind properties."

In 1935, the federal Board of Tax Appeals, a precursor of the federal Tax Court, approved the use of middlemen in the transactions, which made like-kind exchanges far more practical. Then in a court case that reverberated for decades, T. J. Starker and his son and daughter-in-law traded 1,843 acres of Oregon timberland to Crown Zellerbach Corp. in 1967 for a promise to get property (or cash) of equal value five years later.

It was, the Starkers argued, a like-kind exchange with lag, so they said they didn't owe capital gains taxes on the deal in 1967. The Internal Revenue Service disagreed, arguing that waiting five years to make the exchange broke the law. The matter went to court. Twelve years later, a federal appeals court sided with the Starkers, establishing that an exchange didn't have to be simultaneous to qualify for the tax break. Congress later narrowed the window to 180 days.

The result is an industry of middlemen devoted to helping people find property to buy and sell, and matching the transactions in ways that the IRS considers like-kind. One twelve-year-old outfit, Accruit LLC of Denver, secured a patent in 2008 on its method of matching buyers and sellers to assure that their exchanges comply with the tax rules. (In September 2011, Congress said no more patents could be issued for "any strategy for reducing, avoiding or deferring tax liability.")

There are even "reverse exchanges" where–as one 1031 broker describes it on its website–"you can make a new purchase prior to selling the current asset, allowing you to continue generating revenue from your original asset."

Real estate, cable television, and other industries argue that if investors had to pay capital gains taxes, they wouldn't swap one property for another even when the trade made sense, such as for consolidating adjacent cable franchises. Perhaps. But consider this example Accruit posted on its website: Joe and Marilynn Croydon (not their real names) collected and restored vintage cars. A buyer was interested in several of their Formula 1 race cars to the tune of $2.5 million. "After going through countless part orders, mechanic expenses and original purchase prices," the couple figured they would turn a $1.97 million profit–which at the current capital gains tax rate on collectibles meant a tax bill of $552,440. Their accountant recommended a 1031 exchange, and the couple began looking for other cars to buy with the proceeds of the sale.

Eventually they found four of them–a 2008 Lamborghini Reventon ($1.2 million), a 1969 Yenko Camaro ($180,000), a 1981 BMW M1 ($133,500), and a 1933 Duesenberg Model J ($1 million). That more than covered the $2.5 million proceeds. They didn't have to pay the $542,400 in capital gains taxes immediately. And with smart accountants and careful planning, a tax deferred can become a tax never paid. Accruit said in its account that the gains might escape taxation altogether if the cars were bequeathed to the Croydon children.

The tax code has few defenders these days. It's criticized for being too complicated and too onerous, for pushing companies overseas and rewarding them for going abroad, for discouraging saving and restraining growth. In concept, tax reform is popular. But ultimately reforming the tax code turns on some big, contentious issues. Will Congress actually force *anyone* to surrender a cherished provision of the tax code? Will it raise anyone's taxes, even if only to come up with the money to lower taxes for everyone else? Can Republicans and Democrats resolve their standoff over whether the tax code should bring more money to the Treasury in the future than the unreformed tax code would?

CHAPTER 5

WHY THIS CAN'T GO ON FOREVER

Although it is said that the most important things in life cannot be measured, American presidents are judged in real time by numbers, particularly when it comes to the economy. There's the unemployment rate, the one economic statistic everyone instantly understands. And the price of gasoline, the largest price tag on anything sold in the entire country. And the stock market, an instant barometer of the mood of the business and investing class.

Then there's the budget, the national credit card bill. By that metric, where did the United States stand in the fourth year of Barack Obama's presidency? Four years older, and deeper in debt. "We're driving seventy miles an hour toward a cliff," says Bob Reischauer, the former CBO director. "And when we reach that cliff will be determined by events over which we have very little control. The path we're on can't go on for fifteen years. Whether it can go on for two, three, four years, I have no idea."

In Washington, where no one seems to agree on anything these days, substantial agreement actually exists on this assertion. Problem is, there's next to no agreement on *what* to do about it and *when.*

The debate over how to steer the budget has produced a multiact Washington drama for the past couple of years. Act One was the rush to rescue a collapsing economy in 2009 with fiscal stimulus, and the bitterness over bank bailouts. Act Two featured tension among Obama's brainy, big-ego economic advisers about whether to pump more money into the economy and when to shift to worrying about deficits. In Act Three, a procession of bipartisan blue-ribbon groups assembled to seek compromise, none of which forged a consensus broad enough to produce action. Act Four involved a confidence-shaking showdown in August 2011 between the White House and congressional Republicans over raising the ceiling on federal borrowing. And then came Act Five, the legislation that emerged from the showdown that threatens deep, across-the-board spending cuts at the beginning of 2013 unless some deficit-reducing alternative passes before then. In classical tragedy, this is known as the denouement. In Washington, it could be just farce.

Each episode had political consequences, ripples that almost surely will influence the outcome of the 2012 presidential and congressional elections. But in the midst of the political jockeying and brinkmanship, the relevant *economic* consequences of the past four years can be summed up in two fiscal facts. Everything else is pretty much detail.

The first fiscal fact is this:

Obama inherited a collapsing economy. He used substantial fiscal muscle that, with a significant assist from the Federal Reserve, helped arrest that collapse.

A running argument among Obama advisers early in the administration–one that has continued in the after-action books–involves whether the Obama fiscal stimulus *should* or, given political realities, *could* have been bigger than the $787 billion initially approved by Congress in February 2009. There were unending debates about whether the mix of spending increases and tax cuts in that package was optimal: Too much in tax cuts or too little? Too much spending that went instantly into consumers' hands or too much on "shovel-ready" construction projects that took years to launch? The 2012 presidential campaign has homed in on whether the fiscal stimulus did any good at all. Barack Obama said it helped save the United States from repeating the Great Depression. Mitt Romney called it a failure that amounted to "throwing $800 billion out the window."

The fiscal response was big by the standards of history, but then so was the recession. The first shots were fired by what are known in budgetspeak as "automatic stabilizers," the built-in features of the budget that resulted in more spending (because more people were unemployed or eligible for food stamps, for instance) and lower tax receipts (because fewer people had income on which to pay taxes). These added up to well over $300 billion a year for 2009, 2010, and 2011, CBO estimated. Then came the Obama fiscal stimulus–or, as he prefers, "the Recovery Act." CBO's latest price tag on that: $831 billion over a few years, more than initially estimated because the economy was worse, so more were eligible for aid. And then, with the economy still languishing, came the $100-billion-a-year payroll tax holiday for 2011 and 2012, temporarily reducing the payroll taxes workers pay by 2 percentage points.

The argument that such massive spending had *no* impact on the economy at all hasn't much merit. It isn't possible to throw that much money out of the window without someone getting a job and someone spending more than he or she otherwise would. Even Obama critic Douglas Holtz-Eakin, a former McCain adviser who now heads his own center-right think tank, allows, "No one would argue that the stimulus has done nothing." (Never mind that Republican candidates routinely argue just that.)

Yet it's easy to understand why many ordinary citizens see the stimulus as a failure, given how poorly the economy did after the money began to flow. Gauging the impact, measuring the bang for the billions of bucks, requires an exercise with which economists are comfortable and the public isn't—comparing today's economic conditions to what they would have been without the spending increases and tax cuts. "Suppose a patient has been in a terrible accident and has massive internal bleeding," Christina Romer of the University of California at Berkeley told a League of Women Voters audience in August 2011, a year after leaving her post as chair of Obama's White House Council of Economic Advisers. "After life-saving surgery to stop the bleeding, the patient is likely to still feel pretty awful.... But that doesn't mean the surgery didn't work.... Without the surgery the patient would have died. Well, the same is true of the economy back in 2008 and 2009."

Economists like Romer who believe that fiscal stimulus is a potent weapon against unusually severe recessions use economic models and rules of thumb that kick out big beneficial impacts. Witness Harvard's Larry Summers, adviser to Clinton and Obama: "Do you really believe if we had done nothing in response to the crisis in 2008, it would have been a good idea?" But other economists have less faith in fiscal potency, and they produce models that reveal smaller impacts—or even none at all. Witness Stanford's John Taylor, adviser to both Bushes: "They [tax cuts and spending increases of stimulus] wither and they don't give you a lasting recovery," he said. "It goes away and we are even weaker than before."

Though the debate over the efficacy of fiscal stimulus will go on, the consensus among *economists* is that the spending and tax cuts did more than a little good. A February 2012 survey of forty of the biggest names in academic economics ("the world's best economics department," the organizers at the University of Chicago Booth School of Business call it), for instance, found near-unanimity on one point: 90 percent said that unemployment was lower in 2010 than it would have been had there been no stimulus.

Bob Reischauer, seventy, is with the consensus. The physically towering economist, son of prominent Japan scholar Edwin Reischauer, is one of the wise men of budgeting in Washington. Recently retired as head of the Urban Institute think tank, he spent his entire career at CBO–he was one of Alice Rivlin's lieutenants in the agency's infancy–and at Democratic-leaning think tanks in Washington. Reischauer's influence is amplified by his unusual combination of hard-nosed political realism with trenchant economic insight and by reporters' affection for his pithy sound bites. "I'm a believer that Obama saved us from a world depression," he said. "And the American people give him zero credit for that–99 percent of the population has no appreciation for what kind of threat it was." That's an overstatement: the public has warmed to the stimulus as time has passed and the economy has perked up. In a February 2012 Pew poll, 61 percent said it was "mostly good" for the economy, substantially more than the 38 percent who voiced approval two years earlier.

Whatever the merits, that money has been borrowed, and it has been spent–which leads to the second fact:

To rescue the economy, Obama piled more
government debt on top of the debt that he inherited.
He has yet to sell the public or Congress on a credible
plan to avoid unsustainable increases in debt in
the future.

On the day Obama took the oath of office, January 20, 2009, the U.S. government owed $6.3 trillion to others– $6,307,310,739,681.66 to be precise, according to the Treasury's "Debt to the Penny" website. That works out to $54,000 per household or 45 percent of GDP, the yardstick that measures the debt against the size of the whole U.S. economy.

On February 13, 2012, when Obama sent his bud-get to Congress, the government owed $10.6 trillion– $10,596,768,009,341.49. That's $90,000 per household, or nearly 70 percent of GDP, higher than at any time in the past sixty years.

The real problem lies ahead, as Reischauer suggested with his car-at-the-cliff analogy. Obama said as much the day his February 2012 budget was released: "[T]ruth is we're going to have to make some tough choices in order to put this country back on a more sustainable fiscal path. By reducing our deficit in the long term, what that allows us to do is to invest in the things that will help grow our economy right now. We can't cut back on those things that are important for us to grow. We can't just cut our way into growth. We can cut back on the things that we don't need, but we also have to make sure that everyone is paying their fair share for the things that we do need. "

But Obama's latest budget showed that even if Congress accepted every one of his money-saving and tax-increasing proposals and even if his health care law worked as hoped and even if the economy steadily improved, the government would still need to borrow another $4 trillion over the next four years, and the ratio of debt to GDP would keep climbing. And that *doesn't* count trillions more in unfunded promises to pay benefits in the future, which are not formally recorded on the government's books.

ABOUT THE NATIONAL DEBT

For most of recent American history, most U.S. government borrowing was domestic–the Liberty Bonds sold during World War I, War Bonds sold during World War II, the savings bonds that generations of grandparents gave at graduation time, the U.S. Treasury bonds held in Americans' trust accounts and pension funds. "We owe it to ourselves" was the comforting mantra. No longer. Back in 1955, when the federal debt was much smaller, less than 5 percent was held by foreigners. Foreign holdings began to climb in 1970 and surged in the 2000s. Today, foreign governments and private investors hold nearly half of all the U.S. government debt outstanding. A big chunk of this lending is from China and Japan. They have been big

The National Debt

The federal government's debt, measured against the size of the economy, the gross domestic product, has risen to levels that haven't been seen in more than half a century and will keep rising if current policies are pursued.

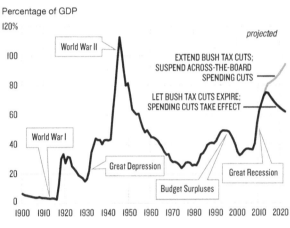

Percentage of GDP

Source: White House Office of Management and Budget

savers, so they have a lot of money to lend to foreigners. And they export a lot more to the United States (when dollars flow into China) than they import (when dollars flow out of China), which leaves them with a growing stockpile of dollars that has to be invested somewhere. The U.S. Treasury bond is still the safest place to put them.

Right now, all this federal government borrowing isn't a problem. While Washington has borrowed heavily over the past few years, consumer and business borrowing has been subdued. Measured as a percentage of GDP, borrowing by the U.S. economy as a whole—not only the federal government but also state and local governments, businesses, and households—

Foreign Debt

A growing fraction of the federal government's borrowing is from abroad, much of it from China and Japan.

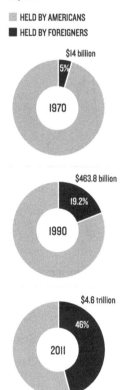

HELD BY AMERICANS

HELD BY FOREIGNERS

$14 billion

5%

1970

$463.8 billion

19.2%

1990

$4.6 trillion

46%

2011

Source: Treasury, White House Office of Management and Budget

peaked in early 2009 and has been falling since. As Massachu-setts Institute of Technology economist Simon Johnson and his co-blogger James Kwak put it in their new book, *White House Burning*: "If the Treasury Department never had to pay interest (and could always borrow as it needed), the national debt would not matter very much."

But the federal government does have to pay interest. Even though the U.S. Treasury borrows more cheaply than almost anyone else on the planet, the U.S. government paid $230 billion in net interest last year, more than triple the $64 billion it spent on all nondefense research and development, from medical research to space exploration. And that's with interest rates at extraordinarily low levels. When rates return to normal, perhaps around 5 percent, each additional $1 trillion in debt will add $50 billion a year to the government's annual interest payments.

And even the mighty U.S. government cannot assume it will always be able to borrow whatever it needs cheaply. The fact that the Chinese, in particular, hold so much of the federal debt–about 25 percent of the debt held by foreigners, according to the U.S. Treasury–conjures up a lot of angst, and that doesn't count the Chinese holdings of debt of Fannie Mae and Freddie Mac, the mortgage lenders backed by the U.S. government. The worry is either that the Chinese will yank all their money out at once (not likely, given that doing so would tank the U.S. economy and with it their investments and exports) or that the reserves give the Chinese leverage over U.S. economic and foreign policies. (They do.) But even if the United States were borrowing from reliable allies, the more borrowed from abroad, the bigger the share of future Americans' income that goes overseas to pay interest and principal.

For all the rhetoric from politicians of both parties about the dangers of debt and deficits, in the end, little was actually done about it in 2011 or 2012. "Kicking the can down the road" became an almost daily mantra in the press, and an accurate one.

One piece of recent legislation took direct aim at the deficit: the Budget Control Act. The law was passed in August 2011 in order to persuade reluctant members of Congress to take the politically unpopular step of voting to raise the ceiling on the federal debt, a bizarre practice in which Congress votes once to spend money and then votes again later to pay the credit card bill when it arrives. Essentially trying to tie its own hands—as it did from 1990 to 2002—Congress set hard ceilings for each of the next ten years on the 40 percent of spending that it appropriates annually, the panoply of domestic and defense items from aircraft carriers to the National Dam Safety Program described in chapter 3 but not Social Security or Medicare or other benefit programs. The caps allow this spending to rise about 2 percent a year, not enough to keep up with expected inflation, which in the world of budgeting is considered a cut of $1 trillion over ten years. If, and it's a big if, the caps hold, spending on everything outside of Social Security, major health programs, and interest would come in below 8 percent of GDP in 2022, lower than at any time in the past forty years.

Congress then took one more step. It pointed a gun at itself (or, if you listen to Panetta, at the Pentagon budget) by mandating further across-the-board defense and domestic spending cuts beginning in January 2013—unless Congress and the president agree on an alternative way to bring projected deficits down by an additional $1.2 trillion over the next ten years. This self-imposed deadline could prompt a significant attack on the deficit some time after the November 2012 elections. Or Congress and the president could undo it, kicking the can down the road again.

WHERE ARE WE NOW?

Each January, the Congressional Budget Office attempts to show where the fiscal ship is headed before Congress tries to steer it with changes to taxes and spending. One telling measure of how contentious budget politics have become is the increasing difficulty of getting agreement even on this starting point, known in Washington as "the baseline." (When there's talk in the newspapers of a $500 billion, ten-year deficit-reduction package, that means some combination of taxes and spending cuts is projected to reduce future deficits by $500 billion from some baseline.)

Crafting baselines has never been easy: they rest on forecasts of everything from the stock market to the number of elderly hips that will be replaced, and those forecasts are certain to be wrong. Understanding baselines hasn't been easy either: if it takes a 4 percent increase in Medicare spending to provide the same services next year as this year, then baseline accounting says that a 3 percent increase in Medicare spending is a 1 percent *cut*. And if that isn't enough to give you a headache, the baseline-making task has grown tougher lately because Congress and presidents have stamped expiration dates on many costly tax and spending programs, and then repeatedly extended them. So should the baseline assume that Medicare spending will go down because the law says doctors' fees will be slashed? Or should it assume that Congress will, as it has to date, waive the fee cuts? Ultimately, what matters is where Congress and the president end up, not where they start. But defining the starting point and crafting the baseline are important to the politics and public perceptions of the budget– they're used by one side to magnify the size of the spending cuts or tax changes proposed by the other side–and politics and perceptions have a lot to do with what actually happens.

Pretending that Congress will let taxes rise and spending fall sharply at the start of 2013 can provide a dangerously misleading picture of the course on which the federal government is set. So the CBO has crafted an alternative. It projects future spending, taxes, and deficits if Congress extends all the Bush tax cuts for everyone at year-end, continues to adjust the pesky alternative minimum tax so it doesn't reach ever deeper into the middle class, and continues to waive the provision in a

1997 deficit-reduction law that would cut Medicare doctor fees. Not everyone likes this approach, but it's a useful road map to where the budget is heading without a course correction.

What does it show? "The good news is that the improving economy will reduce the deficit as a share of GDP considerably over the next few years," said Doug Elmendorf, the current CBO director. As more people get jobs, more tax receipts will flow into the Treasury and spending on unemployment compensation and the like will come down. "The bad news," he continued, "is that the improvement will still leave the deficit so large that, if we maintain our current spending and tax policies, debt will continue to rise sharply, relative to GDP."

In this steady-as-she-goes scenario, spending driven by the aging of the population and rising health costs climbs faster than revenues. A lot faster. Deficits of $1 trillion or more would be the norm, and the national debt would approach 100 percent of GDP within a decade—and climb still higher in the years after that.

No one *really* knows how much the U.S. government can borrow before global investors get uneasy and begin to demand higher interest rates. The national debt exceeded 100 percent of GDP during World War II and then came down as the economy sprinted. But history suggests that debt of that level is in the danger zone. Think Argentina, circa 2001. Think Greece, circa 2012.

"If a country has not balanced its long-run budget when the long run arrives, then the market balances its budget for it–and does so in a way that nobody in the country likes," Brad DeLong, a Berkeley economist and blogger, and a former Clinton adviser, has written. Then he added, drily, "[T]he long run seems to vary between three years and 200 years, depending."

The 2012 election campaign has produced a lot of talk about taxes, spending, and deficits, much of it less than useful in understanding the choices the country faces. Basically, there are three poles in the debate.

The first says: The deficit is a problem. But not now, especially when there is still so much unemployment. The poster boy: Paul Krugman, a Princeton University economist and *New York Times* columnist.

The second says: The deficit is a problem. And the solution is to shrink the government and cut taxes. The poster boy: Paul Ryan, the Republican congressman from Wisconsin and chairman of the House Budget Committee.

The third says: The deficit is a big problem. In fact, it is the "transcendent threat to our economic future." The poster boy: Peter G. Peterson, an octogenarian who is spending a large part of his considerable fortune to warn about the five-alarm fiscal fire ahead.

IT'S UNEMPLOYMENT, STUPID

Paul Krugman is not and probably never will be a policy maker. But he is formidably armed with a Nobel Prize, a perch on the op-ed page of the *New York Times*, and a very sharp pen. Drawn to economics initially by a set of Isaac Asimov's science-fiction novels in which social scientists save the world, Krugman earned his Ph.D. at MIT and won the American Economic Association's prize for the most accomplished economist under forty. Krugman's most noteworthy academic work focuses on international trade and economic geography. Outside the profession, he began to make his mark as a polemicist about twenty years ago and has been writing twice a week for the *Times* since 1999, while blogging in between columns.

Krugman's world is black-and-white: There are good guys and bad guys, smart guys and dumb ones, truth tellers and liars—and most of the bad guys are Republicans. His columns, speeches, and books often offer more ammunition than argument, bolstering those who agree with him rather than changing the minds of those who don't. But compared to other economists and to many policy makers, Krugman saw early how big a blow the economy had suffered. As a result, he advocated for far more fiscal and monetary stimulus than Obama eventually got Congress to approve and Fed chairman Ben Bernanke got his colleagues to pursue. Keynes was right, he shouted. Take his advice.

Rahm Emanuel, Obama's first chief of staff, once dismissed Krugman as economically brilliant and politically naive. "How many bills has he passed?" he asked. To which Krugman replied, "The question is why Obama didn't ask for what the economy needed, then bargain from there."

Krugman's attitude toward the deficit is *fuggedaboutit*. "Premature deficit reduction," he has said, risks "diverting attention from the more immediately urgent task of reducing unemployment." Shouldn't we worry that the rest of the world won't keep lending the U.S. government more money? No, Krugman said. The interest rates that the bond market is charging on long-term loans to the U.S. government suggest that investors aren't worrying about that prospect, so why should the U.S. government? Europe, in his view, provided an instructive case study of misguided fiscal austerity. Countries like Greece that were forced to cut spending aggressively to reduce borrowing strangled their economies and choked off the very growth that would allow them to pay off future debts.

"If we had slashed spending to ward off the invisible bond vigilantes . . . we'd be emulating Europe, and hence emulating Europe's failure," he wrote. We were wise, and we'd be wiser still if we gave the economy another dose of stimulus, he argued.

IT'S SPENDING, STUPID

After Republicans took control of the House, Paul Ryan became chairman of the House Budget Committee, and the most prominent Republican voice on budget matters. His fiscal script, called "A Path to Prosperity," outlined unprecedented changes to the federal budget. Social Security was left alone, but he proposed big changes in the health programs. Federal spending on Medicaid's long-term care coverage would be capped and turned over to the states. Those who turn sixty-five after 2022 would be offered vouchers to buy something resembling today's fee-for-service Medicare or private insurance; to save money, each voucher would be worth less than the CBO currently projects health insurance for the elderly will cost. The notion was that the constraints on spending–"reform," Ryan called it–would force the health care system to get more efficient. Critics said they simply shifted the costs onto the beneficiaries. But that was just a start. Ryan also proposed shrinking the rest of the federal government. Spending on everything outside Social Security, the health insurance programs, and interest would go from 12 percent of GDP in 2010 to 6 percent by 2022, he said, though the outline didn't specify what would be cut.

Unlike the deficit-*über-alles* crowd, Ryan said he wanted to cut taxes, too. Although he didn't offer details–budget resolutions generally don't–he called for lower tax rates for both households and corporations. Backed by economists at the conservative Heritage Foundation (and without the endorsement of the CBO), Ryan predicted a resulting surge in economic growth that would produce enough revenues to reduce future deficits and bring down the debt.

"You shouldn't put yourself in a position of trying to feed ever-higher spending with higher revenues, because you'll never catch up," he argued. His framework rejected what he called the "shared scarcity mentality" of "ever-higher taxes and bureaucratically rationed health care."

Krugman described Ryan's plan as "a strange combination of cruelty and insanely wishful thinking." House Republicans voted for it, but many were uneasy, believing that the far-reaching changes to Medicare (which were altered in the 2012 iteration of the Ryan plan) made them an easy mark for Democrats on the campaign trail.

But Ryan was looking beyond the next election: "I believe the way to make change is to shift the political center of gravity as best you can, by putting ideas out there, solutions out there, and surviving the gauntlet of demagoguery you'll inevitably receive," he said.

IT'S THE DEFICIT, STUPID

If there's a chart or PowerPoint slide that shows a volcano-like explosion of spending or deficits in the future, chances are it was made by, paid for, or inspired by Pete Peterson, age eighty-six, the modern incarnation of an Old Testament prophet roaming the country and the airwaves to lament the profligacy of his times. "My daughter jokes that when I do pass on, it will be at my desk with my head huddled over a speech explaining why the Social Security trust fund is an insolvent oxymoron," he wrote in his memoir. "I hope she's right and that it has lots of PowerPoint charts."

His mission: to generate enough alarm about deficits so politicians cut spending and raise taxes—and soon. Peterson is "the godfather of this whole effort of trying to bring sanity to our nation's finances," said Erskine Bowles, who chaired a deficit-reduction commission that Obama appointed.

Pete Peterson is the son of a Greek immigrant who ran a café in Kearney, Nebraska, that was, Peterson allows, known less for its food than for being open 24/7 for twenty-five uninterrupted years. He hopscotched through corporate America, getting rich along the way. Between stints as chief executive of Bell & Howell and of Lehman Brothers, he served as Nixon's secretary of commerce. In 1985, Peterson cofounded Blackstone Group, a private equity firm, a venture that made him and his partner, Steve Schwarzman, *really* rich.

As Peterson tells it from his office on the forty-eighth floor of a Manhattan office tower with a spectacular view of the New York skyline, his intense focus on the dangers of deficits dates to the early 1980s. He and his wife, his third, were trying to buy a house in East Hampton on Long Island from a friend who was playing hard to get. To win her favor, Peterson agreed to speak at the inaugural forum of a group she was forming, the Women's Economic Round Table. She accepted on the condition that he talk about Ronald Reagan's budget. Peterson had voted for Reagan, assuming him to be both a social and a fiscal conservative, but the homework he did for the speech convinced him otherwise. In March 1981, just two months after Reagan took office, Peterson stunned the White House and Reagan's many fans on Wall Street by condemning his tax cuts as "too much of an all-or-nothing gamble, too much of a high-wire act." The problem, he told the women's roundtable in 1981, was "a growing systemic inability to control mandated [benefit] spending programs." He has been making the same point in speeches, magazine essays, and books for the past thirty years. (And he got the house.)

When Blackstone sold shares to the public in 2007, Peterson cashed out to the tune of $1.85 billion. "I did not want to finish life as the retired CEO playing golf five times a week," he said. He had financed antideficit campaigns before. In 2008, he went big time, creating the Peter G. Peterson Foundation to "engage the American people and our leaders in confronting what I consider to be the greatest challenge before us as a nation: our unsustainable long-term national debt" and endowing it with *$1 billion.*

Peterson's foundation has bankrolled what might be called the deficit-industrial complex, a set of overlapping organizations with a shared goal of rallying the public—and especially the business and political elite—to reduce the deficit before financial Armageddon arrives. In 2011, the foundation gave $3.1 million to an outfit formed by a passionate deficit warrior, David Walker, a former head of the Government Accountability Office and also an ex–chief executive of the Peterson Foundation; $1.5 million to the Concord Coalition, a group Peterson helped form in the 1990s that, among other things, runs a roving "fiscal wake-up tour" to get the public alarmed; more than $500,000 to the Committee for a Responsible Federal Budget, a nonpartisan Washington group that presses the case for deficit reduction; and $200,000 each to six think tanks of differing political persuasions to craft deficit-reduction plans of their own. The foundation has financed an eighty-five-minute documentary on the dangers of debt, called *I.O.U.S.A.* It has run a national advertising campaign around a fictional presidential candidate named "Hugh Jidette." (Say it quickly three times.) Because Pete Peterson likes them, the foundation also produces a steady stream of scary and colorful charts.

The message is simple and consistent: the United States must slay the deficit dragon before it kills the United States. The actual belt-tightening should be delayed until the economy has recovered, but it must be done if the nation is to make the investments needed to restore the American dream of rising living standards.

"On our current course, we are headed toward an unthinkable situation in which the federal government spends more than four times as much on interest as it spends on education, R&D, and infrastructure, combined," Pete Peterson has said. "This effectively would mean spending much more on our past than we do on our future... robbing future generations of the opportunities we have enjoyed." And in contrast to Paul Ryan—and current Republican orthodoxy—Peterson has long argued that tax increases are essential, inevitable, *and* wise. "Unlike some of my Wall Street colleagues," Peterson wrote in the *Atlantic* back in October 1993 and has repeated frequently ever since, "I see absolutely nothing wrong with imposing higher tax burdens on the wealthiest in our society."

A TWO-FISTED FISCAL POLICY

Inside the White House, the banner for doing more, much more, to help the economy than Obama and Congress did was carried by Christina Romer, the Berkeley economist and chair of the Council of Economic Advisers. The CEA is an unusual cog in the economic-policy-making apparatus. Created by Congress in 1946, the three-member council of economists, usually drawn from academia, controls nothing. Its sole task is to give the president "objective economic advice and analysis." Its influence varies from administration to administration, and its fiscal advice over the years is a history of the evolution of economists' thinking about budgets.

Romer is a numbers-crunching bleeding heart. "The first recession I really remember was that in 1981–82," she once said. "That recession was personal." In 1983, her father lost his engineering job at a chemical company. "I vividly remember the phone call where he told me that he had 'been sacked.' He was careful to say that I shouldn't worry about my wedding, which was scheduled for that summer. There was money put aside for that." Her father later found a lower-paying, though stable, job overseeing subway car rehabilitation in Philadelphia.

Romer drew unwelcome notoriety early in the administration when she and a colleague predicted in January 2009 that, without any stimulus, the unemployment rate would reach 9 percent but an $800 billion dose of fiscal adrenaline would keep it from rising above 8 percent. As later revisions to government data revealed, the economy was in much worse shape at that moment than the Obama team realized. Still, unemployment peaked at 10 percent in October 2009, and Republicans have never let her forget the flawed prediction.

Romer shared Krugman's frustration that the government wasn't doing more to bring down unemployment–and still does. "The evidence is stronger than it has ever been that fiscal policy matters–that fiscal stimulus helps the economy add jobs and that reducing the budget deficit lowers growth, at least in the near term," she said after leaving the White House. In the early days of the Obama administration, she saw a case for a much bigger fiscal stimulus (as much as $1.8 trillion) than the new president eventually proposed. She believes the economy would be better today if Obama had secured another big dose of stimulus in late 2009.

But she doesn't share Krugman's conviction that the deficit can be safely ignored for now, especially in the wake of the tumult in Europe over governments that can't pay their debts. In fact, the *only* way, in her view, to get more stimulus now is to package it with a credible set of deficit-reducing measures that would take effect later when the economy was stronger. "We don't have to reduce the deficit immediately. In fact, we can increase it temporarily, as we need to, to help create jobs," she has said. "But to reassure financial markets (and ourselves) that we will be solvent over the long haul, we need to pass a plan as soon as possible for reducing the deficit gradually over time."

Although less emphatic in public, Fed chairman Bernanke takes a similar view. He is wary about prescribing fiscal policy to members of Congress, who like to remind him that decisions on taxes and spending are their turf, not his. But when pressed at a February 2012 hearing in the House, he endorsed what he called "a two-handed plan"—one that coupled increased spending on infrastructure or education or tax cuts while simultaneously addressing "the long-term necessity of making fiscal policy sustainable.... You need to think about those two things together."

Alas, thinking about "two things together" is not Congress's strength. In their rhetoric for much of the past couple of years, both Congress and the president have rushed to one side (extend the Bush income tax cuts, continue payroll tax holidays, cut corporate tax rates) and then to the other (raise taxes on the rich, close tax loopholes, cap annually appropriated spending, slow the growth in Medicare spending). Obama's latest budget has elements of both: a proposal, for instance, for a new tax break to encourage employers to hire (would in-crease the deficit by $14 billion in the first year) and a proposal to limit the tax deductions for upper-income taxpayers (would reduce the deficit by $27 billion in the first year). Republicans promptly chastised him for seeking to raise taxes and cut spending on Medicare, and then complained he wasn't doing anything about the deficit.

THE TRUTH TELLER

Romer and Ryan, Krugman and Peterson are full-throated ad-vocates with clear and loudly stated views on what the gov-ernment should and shouldn't do differently. In contrast, Doug Elmendorf, director of the CBO, is more of a national truth teller, trying to make the public and the politicians understand choices they cannot evade while at the same time not hurting his—and the CBO's—credibility by taking sides. The *Washington Examiner* once dubbed him "a geek with guts." At a time when almost every fact about the federal budget is the subject of fierce debate, Elmendorf's measured voice can be hard to hear, but some people do listen. When he called a press briefing on the agency's annual economic and budget outlook in January 2012, he drew ten television cameras to record his carefully calibrated words.

Slim and bespectacled, Elmendorf could play a college professor on TV. "A quiet man who thinks carefully about everything," the *New York Times* once said of him. Indeed, he deliberately chose a baseball game for one of his first dates with his future wife. "You want to be sure there's something going on to fill the lull in the conversation but not like a movie where you can't talk," he explained.

Elmendorf's academic pedigree is impeccable: Princeton, 1983; Harvard Ph.D., 1989. The advisers for his dissertation– "Fiscal Policy and Financial Markets"–were Martin Feldstein and Greg Mankiw, top economic advisers, respectively, to Reagan and George W. Bush, and Larry Summers, top economic adviser to Clinton and Obama. After five years helping to teach the big introductory economics course at Harvard, Elmendorf came to Washington in the mid-1990s to work at the CBO. "Starting about then," he said, "I thought being CBO director would be a very good job." But first he went to work on the staff of the Federal Reserve Board, with a couple of breaks to work on the staffs of the White House Council of Economic Advisers and the Clinton Treasury. Elmendorf left government in 2007 for the Brookings Institution think tank but came back in 2009 when the congressional leadership–then all Democrats–picked him to run the CBO, succeeding Peter Orszag, who went to the White House to be Obama's budget director.

At congressional hearings, Elmendorf is like the referee in a food fight. With calm dispassionate words and charts, he tries to give his bosses in Congress a reality check. Members of Congress cross-examine Elmendorf as if he were an expert witness in a murder trial, laboring to get him to support the questioner's point of view. (Senator Kent Conrad, a Democrat from North Dakota, at a February 2012 hearing: "Why wouldn't one conclude from what you've said here that the best policy in the short term would be to extend tax cuts, at least some significant part of the tax cuts, and defer some of the spending cuts... several years, but right now agree to a plan that will raise revenue and cut spending so that at the end of the 10 years we've dramatically reduced deficits and reduced the growth of debt?")

Elmendorf tries just as hard to be sure Congress understands the daunting dimensions of the deficit and the alternative ways to reduce it while avoiding taking sides in the partisan debate, particularly over taxes. ("I don't want to speak to a specific combination of policies that the Congress might choose to extend or let expire," he told Conrad. "But on your general point, I think agreement about how the country's budget will be put on a sustainable path would be a good thing for the economy in the short run because it would give people some confidence that they knew where policies were headed, which is very hard to have in the current environment.")

Elmendorf, in short, is a good guide to the fiscal landscape. His tour begins with a couple of observations.

One is a demographic fact. "We cannot go back to the tax and spending policies of the past because the number of people sixty-five or older will increase by one-third between 2012 and 2022," Elmendorf says. As more baby boomers cross the threshold for collecting Social Security or being covered by Medicare, spending on those programs will rise. And even hard-core spending cutters willing to talk about paring Social Security or Medicare or raising the eligibility age propose exempting those who have already turned fifty-five.

The other is a political fact that sums up the entire budget dilemma in a single sentence. "The country faces a fundamental disconnect between the services the people expect the government to provide, particularly in the form of benefits for older Americans, and the tax revenues that people are willing to send to the government to finance those services," he has said.

The CBO's traditional role is to take budget plans that the president and members of Congress devise and put numbers on them: what would the course of spending and taxes and deficits be if they were enacted. To that end, it also produces a Chinese menu of deficit-reducing options from which Congress can choose.

But none of that seemed to be penetrating the political debate. So Elmendorf tried a different tack. He started by projecting today's tax and spending policies ten years out, the baseline referred to earlier. That would put the budget deficit in 2022 above $1 trillion and rising. By then, the U.S. government would be borrowing so much that the national debt, as a percentage of the GDP, would be dangerously high (over 90 percent) and still rising.

Then he asked: What would have to happen to avoid that outcome, to bring the spending and revenue lines close enough together so that the national debt would at least stop climbing, as a percentage of GDP? His answer: spending cuts or tax increases or a combination of the two that add up to $750 billion a year by 2022. Even in Washington that's a big number.

What would it take to get to that goal? Remember, the starting point for the exercise is that Congress sticks to the caps it has set on annually appropriated defense and domestic spending. "The country," Elmendorf pointed out, "is [already] on track to substantially reduce the role of most federal activities, relative to the size of the economy." Perhaps Congress will squeeze more out of defense between now and 2022, depending on the state of the world. But it's a good bet that what it saves in defense, it'll end up spending on domestic programs–highways or job training or disaster relief or something.

So say Congress decided to get really serious about the deficit by looking at spending on the big benefit programs that today account for 40 percent of all federal outlays: Social Security and the growing Medicare and Medicaid budgets. Say it raised the age at which the elderly become eligible for Medicare to sixty-seven (from sixty-five) and the age at which they're eligible for full Social Security benefits to seventy (from sixty-seven). Say it shifted to a less generous formula for setting Social Security benefits and adjusting them for inflation. Say it boosted the premiums that the elderly on Medicare pay for their coverage and made them pay more of their health care bills out of pocket. And say it limited increases in federal spending for Medicaid, the joint state-federal health insurance program for the poor, so the tab rose no faster than the pace at which private sector wages rise.

Any one of those would be a very big deal. But if Congress did all that, it would be saving about $250 billion annually by 2022. That's a big number to be sure, but here's the rub: all those measures combined would save only a third of what's needed to reach Elmendorf's budget nirvana goal. If *all* the weight is put on the big entitlement programs—Social Security, Medicare, and Medicaid—they would need to be cut by 25 percent to put the budget on a sustainable course by 2022.

Which is why the conversation inevitably turns to raising taxes alongside cutting spending.

Elmendorf's starting point for the exercise is that all the tax cuts that Bush instigated and Obama continued are extended at the end of the year. Say Congress took Obama's advice and let income tax rates on the over-$250,000-a-year crowd rise to pre-Bush levels. That would bring in between $100 billion and $150 billion in 2020. Say it also eliminated the federal income tax deductions for mortgage interest and state and local taxes, changes that would raise taxes on many more people. That would yield another $180 billion. Both would be huge changes, and they, too, would get Congress only about one-third of the way toward the goal. If Social

Security, Medicare, and Medicaid were shielded altogether, then taxes would have to be raised by about one-sixth. That's a big tax increase.

Put all the spending cuts and the tax increases on this shopping list into the deficit-reduction basket, and there still would not be enough money to bring the deficit to sustainable levels by 2022. Elmendorf's list of options is hardly exhaustive: if Congress let *all* the Bush tax cuts expire, raising the taxes of almost everyone who pays income taxes, it would, by CBO estimates, come close to hitting the target. But the point is clear: small changes will *not* suffice.

That's not to say that the nation's fiscal problem is unsolvable. The proliferation of reports by bipartisan commissions illustrates the mix of significant, but manageable, policies that could arrest the rise in the federal debt over the next decade. Most of them raise some taxes by eliminating deductions, credits, loopholes, and exemptions; cut the defense budget; restrain spending on health and other benefits; and spread the pain widely while trying to shield the poorest Americans. Yet the polarization of the American political system has left it, so far, unable to choose between Barack Obama's approach to reducing the deficit or Paul Ryan's. Neither side has enough votes to prevail, and neither is willing to compromise on some amalgam that might spread the pain and that both can live with. This is the crux of the issue: the deficit widens, the debt grows, the interest burden gets heavier, the voices grow even more shrill as the budget burden is passed to future generations, and nothing gets done.

"I used to tell the students that we are either governed by leadership or crisis," Leon Panetta said in a recent interview. "And I always thought that if leadership wasn't there, then ultimately you rely on crisis to drive decisions. In the last few years, my biggest concern is that crisis doesn't seem to drive decisions either. So there goes my theory."

NOTES

CHAPTER 1: SPENDING $400 MILLION AN HOUR

16 "broken promises": Paul Ryan press release, February 13, 2012. http://budget.house.gov/News/DocumentSingle .aspx?DocumentID=280066

16 "I have a soft spot": Interview, Jack Lew.

17 "The purpose of power": Tim Weiner, "Old-Time Democrat Tries to Weave a Budget Tapestry," Public Lives, *New York Times*, November 8, 1999. http://www.nytimes .com/1999/11/08/us/public-lives-old-time-democrat -tries-to-weave-a-budget-tapestry.html

17 Eleven days after: "Paul Ryan: Rebel Without a Pause," *Wisconsin Policy Research Institute,* July 2010. http://www .wpri.org/WIInterest/Vol19No2/Schneider19.2p2.html

18 "I do believe": Jennifer Rubin, "Making the Case for Free Markets and Profit," washingtonpost.com, January 12, 2012. http://www.washingtonpost.com/blogs/ right-turn/post/making-the-case-for-free-markets-and -profit/2012/01/11/gIQAX9zVrP_blog.html

18 "It cost me": Ezra Klein, "Rep. Paul Ryan: Rationing Happens Today! The Question Is Who Will Do It?,"

washingtonpost.com, February 2, 2010. http://voices .washingtonpost.com/ezra-klein/2010/02/rep_paul _ryan_rationing_happen.html

18 One liberal group: Paul Ryan Wheelchair Commercial, The Agenda Project, May 17, 2011. http://www.politi fact.com/truth-o-meter/statements/2011/may/25/ agenda-project/throw-granny-cliff-ad-says-paul-ryan -plan-would-pr/

19 "Byrd droppings": Mary Agnes Carey, "How the Senate Will Tackle Health Care Reform," *Kaiser Health News,* March 21, 2010. http://www.kaiserhealthnews.org/Sto-ries/2010/March/22/Senate-health-bill-whats-next.aspx

19 CHIMPS: Jim Monke, "Reductions in Mandatory Agriculture Program Spending," Congressional Research Service (Washington, D.C.: May 19, 2010). http://www .nationalaglawcenter.org/assets/crs/R41245.pdf

19 As humor columnist: David Wessel, "Deficit Dilemma: How to Dig Out," *Wall Street Journal,* October 15, 2009, A2. http://online.wsj.com/article/SB125554787267585505 .html

21 "In 2009, for the first time": Interview, Eugene Steuerle.

21 The United States spends: http://milexdata.sipri.org/ files/?file=SIPRI+milex+data+1988-2010.xls

22 Yet in a CNN poll: CNN Opinion Research Poll, March 11-13, 2011. http://i2.cdn.turner.com/cnn/2011/ images/03/31/rel4m.pdf

22 Wages and benefits: Office of Management and Budget, *Fiscal Year 2013 Analytical Perspectives* (Washington, D.C.: Government Printing Office, 2012), Table 11-4.

22 4.4 million workers: Ibid., Table 11-3.

22 Where does the rest of the money go?: Office of Man-agement and Budget, *Historical Tables* (Washington, D.C.:

Government Printing Office, 2012), Tables 11–3, 12–1. http://www.whitehouse.gov/omb/budget/Historicals

23 "It's the things:" Interview.

23 The heart of federal health care spending: Congressional Budget Office, *Long-Term Budget Outlook* (Washington, D.C.: Government Printing Office, 2012), Figure B-1. http://www.cbo.gov/doc.cfm?index=12212

24 The Medicare prescription drug benefit: David Wessel, "Tallying the Toll of Terrorism on the Economy from 9/11," *Wall Street Journal*, September 1, 2011, A2.

24 "You can't fix": Interview at WSJ CEO Council.

24 wiped out $7 trillion: http://www.newyorkfed.org/research/staff_reports/sr482.pdf

25 "At one point": http://cybercemetery.unt.edu/archive/cop/20110401232213/http:/cop.senate.gov/documents/cop-031611-report.pdf

25 only $470 billion: U.S. Department of Treasury, "Troubled Asset Relief Program (TARP)–Monthly Report to Congress," April 10, 2012. http://www.treasury.gov/initiatives/financial-stability/briefing-room/reports/105/Documents105/March%2012%2Report/%2010%20Congress.pdf

26 As of December 2011: Federal Housing Financing Agency, *Conservator's Report on the Enterprises Financial Condition, Fourth Quarter 2011*. http://www.fhfa.gov/webfiles/23879/Conservator%27sReport4Q201141212F.pdf

27 for families in the very middle: Congressional Budget Office, "Trends in Federal Tax Revenues and Rates," December 2, 2010, 2. http://www.cbo.gov/publication/21938

27 Nearly half of American households: Rachel M. Johnson et al., "Why Some Tax Units Pay No Income Tax," Tax Policy Center, July 27, 2011. http://www.taxpolicycenter.org/publications/url.cfm?ID=1001547

28 less than a third of the populace: Bureau of the Census, "Income, Poverty, and Health Insurance Coverage in the United States: 2010," September 2011, 23. http://www .census.gov/prod/2011pubs/p60-239.pdf

28 government at all levels: Organization for Economic Cooperation and Development, *Revenue Statistics 2011* (Paris: OECD Publishing, 2011), 19.

28 All these tax breaks: Office of Management and Budget, *Fiscal Year 2013 Analytical Perspectives*, "Estimates of Total Income Tax Expenditures for Fiscal Years 2011–2017," Table 17–1.

30 U.S. government borrowed: Office of Management and Budget, *Historical Tables*, Table 8–1.

32 "A lot of us": Interview, Erskine Bowles.

CHAPTER 2: HOW WE GOT HERE

33 "This country cannot": Leon E. Panetta, Speech at the Commonwealth Club of California, October 23, 2009. http://www.5min.com/Video/CIA-Director-Calls -Deficit-a-Threat-to-National-Security-516897448

34 "a dangerous experiment": Testimony, Leon E. Panetta, Senate Committee on Government Affairs, January 11, 1993. http://www.archive.org/stream/nominationofleon 00unit/nominationofleon00unit_djvu.txt

35 "I've become very eclectic": Interview, Leon Panetta.

35 A natural politician: "The Defense Secretary: Leon Panetta," *60 Minutes*, January 29, 2012. http://www .cbsnews.com/8301-18560_162-57367997/the-defense -secretary-an-interview-with-leon-panetta/?tag=content Main;cbsCarousel

37 Every week: 2011 Annual Report of the Boards of Trust-

ees of the Federal Hospital Insurance and Federal Supplementary Medical Insurance Trust Funds, May 11, 2011, 51. https://www.cms.gov/ReportsTrustFunds/downloads/tr2011.pdf

37 Back then, the entire output: Louis Johnston and Samuel H. Williamson, "What Was the U.S. GDP Then?," MeasuringWorth, 2011. http://www.measuringworth.com/usgdp/

38 Until Congress created: *United States Government Manual,* 1945. http://www.ibiblio.org/hyperwar/ATO/USGM/Executive.html

38 "The first requirement": Herbert Stein, *The Fiscal Revolution in America: Policy in Pursuit of Reality* (Washington, D.C.: American Enterprise Institute Press, 1996), 33.

38 About 70 percent: Office of Management and Budget, *Historical Tables* (Washington, D.C., Government Printing Office, 2012), 7.

38 "The federal budget": Stein, *Fiscal Revolution in America,* 14.

38 "Too often": Quoted in Stein, 44.

39 "Spending," Stein wrote: Ibid., 54.

39 Largely because of: Bureau of the Census, "District of Columbia–Race and Hispanic Origin: 1800 to 1990," Table 23. http://www.census.gov/population/www/documentation/twps0056/tab23.pdf

40 In a move with: Philip R. Dame and Bernard H. Martin, *The Evolution of OMB* (Washington, D.C.: privately published, 2009), 9. Also see Franklin D. Roosevelt, Exec. Order No. 8248: Reorganizing the Executive Office of the President, September 8, 1939. http://www.presidency.ucsb.edu/ws/index.php?pid=15808#ixzz1maeq2AWc

40 "Never again": Stein, 54.

41 "In three short years": Governor Mitch Daniels's Republican response to the 2012 State of the Union, January 24, 2012. http://www.speaker.gov/News/DocumentSingle .aspx?DocumentID=276315

41 "From the mid-1930s": Interview.

42 "My dad used to": "The Defense Secretary," *60 Minutes,* transcript, 2. http://www.cbsnews.com/8301-18560_162 -57367997/the-defense-secretary-an-interview-with -leon-panetta/?tag=contentMain;cbsCarousel

42 "I had read about": Leon Panetta Interview, Conversations with History, Institute of International Studies, UC Berkeley, May 22, 2000, 243. http://globetrotter.berkeley. edu/people/Panetta/panetta-con2.html

43 Frank Lichtenberg estimates: Frank R. Lichtenberg, "The Effects of Medicare on Health Care Utilization and Outcomes," January 2002. http://www.nber.org/ chapters/c9857.pdf

44 It's a living laboratory: David Wessel, "Medicare Cures: Easy to Prescribe, Tricky to Predict," *Wall Street Journal,* June 30, 2003, A1.

44 "the man who blew": Leon E. Panetta and Peter Gall, *Bring Us Together: The Nixon Team and the Civil Rights Retreat* (New York: J. B. Lippincott Co., 1971). http://www .amazon.com/Bring-together-Nixon-rights-retreat/dp/ B000CKH9Q

45 Congress hasn't finished: Gregory Korte, "Congress Looks at Ways to Fix Budget Process," *USA Today,* October 4, 2011. http://www.usatoday.com/news/washing ton/story/2011-10-03/congress-examines-budget -process/50647934/1

45 But in a city riddled: David Wessel, "Man Who Wounded Health Care Effort Could Also Save It," *Wall Street Jour-*

nal, July 23, 2009, A4. http://online.wsj.com/article/
SB124829913479973605.html

46 "who can grasp": Philip G. Joyce, *The Congressional Budget Office: Honest Numbers, Power and Policymaking* (Washington, D.C.: Georgetown University Press, 2011), 20, 388.

46 "Congress would have a bill": Ibid., 20.

46 "on the explicit grounds": Hali J. Edison, "An Interview with Alice Rivlin." http://www.cswep.org/rivlin.htm

47 "schmoozy": Peter Suderman, "The Gatekeeper," *Reason,* January 2010. http://reason.com/archives/2009/12/08/the-gatekeeper/singlepage

47 "Elmendorf... is the stone-faced banker": RJ Eskow, "Elmendor vs. Orszag: A 'Teachable Moment' . . . for Geeks and Nerds," July 28, 2009. http://www.huffing tonpost .com/rj-eskow/elmendorf-vs-orszag-a-tea_b_246672 .html

48 "In the end, everyone": Interview, Douglas Holtz-Eakin.

48 "To a degree": Allen Schick, *The Federal Budget: Politics, Policy, Process* (Washington, D.C.: The Brookings Institution, 2000), 19–20.

48 for the first time: George Hager and Eric Pianin, *Mirage: Why Neither Democrats nor Republicans Can Balance the Budget, End the Deficit, and Satisfy the Public* (New York: Times Books/Henry Holt, 1997), 97.

49 "Well, you know": Ronald Reagan, quoted in Bruce Bartlett, " 'Starve the Beast': Origins and Development of a Budgetary Metaphor," *The Independent Review,* Summer 2007, 11. http://www.independent.org/pdf/tir/tir _12_01_01_bartlett.pdf

49 "If you insisted": David Stockman, *The Triumph of Politics* (New York: Harper & Row, 1986), 53.

50 "Two Santa Claus Theory": See Jude Wanniski, "Taxes and a Two-Santa Theory," *National Observer,* March 6, 1976. http://capitalgainsandgames.com/blog/bruce-bart lett/1701/jude-wanniski-taxes-and-two-santa-theory.

51 "At that point": Interview, Leon Panetta.

51 The Reagan tax cut was gigantic: Office of Tax Analysis, "Revenue Effects of Major Tax Bills–Updated Tables for All 2010 Bills." http://www.treasury.gov/resource -center/tax-policy/Documents/OTA-Rev-Effects-1940 -present-6-6-2011.pdf

51 "If the American political system": Richard Darman, *Who's in Control? Polar Politics and the Sensible Center* (New York: Simon & Schuster, 1996), 79.

51 "$200 billion a year": Steven R. Weisman, "Budget Tie-up: Reagan at the Crossroads," *New York Times,* April 20, 1983.

52 the budget deficit averaged: Office of Management and Budget, *Historical Tables* (Washington, D.C.: Government Printing Office, 2012), Table 1.2.

52 "A significant tax cut": http://globetrotter.berkeley.edu/ people/Panetta/panetta-con0.html

52 "the six most destructive words": Colin MacKenzie, "How Bush Blew It," *Globe and Mail,* November 4, 1992, A1.

53 "a borrow, bailout, and buy-out binger": Leon Panetta, speech to the National Press Club, January 17, 1989, in *Congressional Record,* January 20, 1989.

53 "Both Democrats and Republicans": http://globetrotter .berkeley.edu/people/Panetta/panetta-con0.html

54 "The American people": "Budget Plan Nears Vote in House," *Chicago Tribune,* October 28. 1990, C17.

54 The vote tally: http://www.govtrack.us/congress/vote .xpd?vote=h1990-528

55 "For Democrats": Interview, Leon Panetta.

55 "undermined": Andrew Rosenthal, "The 1992 Campaign: Breaking Tax Pledge Hurt His Credibility, President Tells ABC." *New York Times,* June 26, 1992. http://www.nytimes.com/1992/06/26/us/the-1992-campaign-breaking-tax-pledge-hurt-his-credibility-president-tells-abc.html

55 "The record shows": http://www.thefiscaltimes.com/Articles/2010/06/25/A-Budget-Deal-That-Did-Reduce-the-Deficit.aspx#page1

56 "The Soviet Union": Interview, Robert Reischauer.

56 "I think the most dangerous threat": Craig Whitlock, "Former Deficit Hawk Leon Panetta Now Fights Budget Cuts as Defense Secretary," *Washington Post,* November 3, 2011. http://www.washingtonpost.com/world/national-security/leon-panettas-mind-meld/2011/10/26/gIQAhtU4iM_story.html

57 "We talked": "Conversations with History," Institute of International Studies, University of California, Berkeley, 2000. http://globetrotter.berkeley.edu/people/Panetta/panetta-con0.html

58 The deficit came down even faster: http://www.cbo.gov/ftpdocs/103xx/doc10392/1993_09_14reischauer testimony.pdf

58 In 1995, the IRS counted: David Wessel, "The Wealth Factor: Again, the Rich Get Richer, but This Time They Pay More Taxes–Their Deductions Are Cut, and That Pesky Levy for Medicare Adds Up–a Big Break on Capital Gains," *Wall Street Journal,* April 2, 1998, A1.

58 "You know . . . does it really hurt": U.S. House of Representatives, Committee on the Budget, *Hearings on President Clinton's Fiscal Year 1995 Budget Proposal,* February 4,

1994, serial no. 103–18 (Washington, D.C.: Government Printing Office, 1994), 42, 45.

59 "In the time that I've been in Washington": http://www .pbs.org/newshour/bb/white_house/january97/ panetta_1-17.html.

60 "We know big government": State of the Union address, January 23, 1996. http://clinton4.nara.gov/WH/New/ other/sotu.html

60 "Leon [Panetta] and John Kasich": Interview, Jack Lew.

61 "Gingrich wanted to do it": http://www.usnews.com/ news/politics/articles/2008/05/29/the-pact-between -bill-clinton-and-newt-gingrich

61 "Why would we go back": Interview, Grover Norquist.

62 "[T]he highly desirable": Testimony of Alan Greenspan, Senate Budget Committee, January 25, 2001.

62 "a feeding frenzy": Alan Greeenspan, *The Age of Turbulence: Adventures in a New World* (New York: Penguin Press, 2007).

62 "misjudged the emotions": Ibid., 222.

62 "policies that could": Testimony of Alan Greenspan, Senate Budget Committee, January 25, 2001.

64 *$3.3 trillion:* http://www.cbo.gov/ftpdocs/121xx/doc 12187/ChangesBaselineProjections.pdf

64 the government spent more: http://cboblog.cbo.gov/?p =3058

66 "The era of big government": David Wessel, "Capital: Small-Government Rhetoric Gets Filed Away," *Wall Street Journal,* September 8, 2005, A2.

66 In 2011, it was 5 percent: Office of Management and Budget, *Historical Tables,* Tables 8.2 and 8.4.

67 By 2010, the *annual* tab: https://www.cms.gov/Reports TrustFunds/downloads/tr2011.pdf, 9, 34.

67 "[A]fter Democrats": "Remarks by the President on Fiscal Policy," April 13, 2011. http://www.whitehouse.gov/the-press-office/2011/04/13/remarks-president-fiscal-policy

68 "would never again permit": http://www.scribd.com/doc/18757758/Pa-Nett-at-Ask-Force-Testimony-October-2007

CHAPTER 3: WHERE THE MONEY GOES

69 The *instructions*: White House, "Preparation, Submission, and Execution of the Budget." http://www.whitehouse.gov/omb/circulars_a11_current_year_a11_toc

69 The Department of Homeland Security's: "U.S. Department of Homeland Security Annual Performance Report: Fiscal Years 2011–2013." http://www.dhs.gov/xlibrary/assets/mgmt/dhs-congressional-budget-justification-fy2013.pdf

70 The typical respondent: CNN Opinion Research Poll, March 11–13, 2011. http://i2.cdn.turner.com/cnn/2011/images/03/31/rel4m.pdf

70 a 2008 Cornell University: Suzanne Mettler, "Reconstituting the Submerged State: The Challenges of Social Policy Reform in the Obama Era." *Perspective on Politics* 8, no. 3 (September 2010): 809. http://government.arts.cornell.edu/assets/faculty/docs/mettler/submerged stat_mettler.pdf

71 When Gallup asked: Jeffrey M. Jones, "Americans Say Federal Gov't Wastes over Half of Every Dollar," September 19, 2011. http://www.gallup.com/poll/149543/americans-say-federal-gov-wastes-half-every-dollar.aspx

71 unused wireless devices: Office of Management and Budget, "Cuts, Consolidations and Savings," 144. http://www.whitehouse.gov/sites/default/files/omb/budget/fy2013/assets/ccs.pdf

71 the *Washington Post* identified: David S. Fallis, Scott Higham, and Kimberly Kindy, "Congressional Earmarks Sometimes Used to Fund Projects Near Lawmakers' Properties," *Washington Post,* February 6, 2012. http://www.washingtonpost.com/investigations/2012/01/12/gIQA97HGvQ_story.html?hpid=z1

71 Social Security Administration: Office of Management and Budget, "Cuts, Consolidations and Savings," 150. http://www.whitehouse.gov/sites/default/files/omb/budget/fy2013/assets/ccs.pdf

71 "Reducing the deficit": Interview, Stan Collender.

72 "My goal was": Interview, Rob Portman.

76 "It is the aging": House Budget Committee, The Congressional Budget Office's Budget and Economic Outlook Hearing, February 1, 2012.

76 Between 1999 and 2009: : Agency for Healthcare Research and Quality, H-CUPnet. http://hcupnet.ahrq.gov/

76 In 2009, Medicare spent: Government Accountability Office, *Medicare: Lack of Price Transparency May Hamper Hospitals' Ability to Be Prudent Purchasers of Implantable Medical Devices* (Washington, D.C.: January 2012).

78 Under the new system: Congressional Budget Office, "Reducing the Deficit: Spending and Revenue Options," March 2011, 55. http://www.cbo.gov/ftpdocs/120xx/doc12085/03-10-ReducingTheDeficit.pdf. See also Medicare Payment Advisory Commission, "Health Care Spending and the Medicare Program," June 2011, 167. http://www

.medpac.gov/documents/Jun11DataBookEntireReport
.pdf

79 The White House budget office: Office of Management
and Budget, *Fiscal Year 2013 Budget,* 227.

81 "When Republicans seized": Michael Grunwald,
"Why Our Farm Policy Is Failing," *Time,* November 7,
2007. http://www.time.com/time/magazine/article/
0,9171,1680139,00.html

81 "an entitlement tied": Dan Morgan, "The Farm Bill
and Beyond" (Washington, D.C.: The German Mar-
shall Fund, 2010), 13. http://209.200.80.89/publications/
article.cfm?id=781&parent_type=P

81 Half of the direct: Office of Management and Budget,
Fiscal Year 2013 Budget, 28. http://www.whitehouse.gov/
sites/default/files/omb/budget/fy2013/assets/cutting
.pdf

82 the first congressional district: Environmental Working Group, 2011 Farm Subsidy Database. http://farm
.ewg.org/progdetail.php?fips=00000&progcodeotal
_dp&page=district&regionname heUnitedStates

82 half of the money: Ibid.

82 "no longer defensible": Office of Management and Budget, "Cuts, Consolidations and Savings," 29. http://www
.whitehouse.gov/sites/default/files/omb/budget/
fy2013/assets/ccs.pdf

82 "Everybody needs to share": http://www.kansas.com/
2011/06/14/1891504/payments-to-farmers-likely-to
.html

82 tab to the taxpayer: Office of Management and Budget,
Fiscal Year 2013 Budget (Washington, D.C.,: Government
Printing Office, 2012), 28.

83 "the food-stamp president": Damian Paletta, "Campaign Renews Scrutiny of Growing Food-Stamp Program," wsj .com, January 17, 2012. http://blogs.wsj.com/economics/ 2012/01/17/campaign-renews-scrutiny-of-growing -food-stamp-program/

83 "wants us to become": Interview, Fox News, January 16, 2012. http://www.foxnews.com/on-air/hannity/2012/ 01/17/romney-sticks-story-super-pac-ads-post-sc-debate-interview

83 as of December 2011: USDA, "Supplemental Nutrition Assistance Program." http://www.fns.usda.gov/pd/ 34SNAPmonthly.htm

84 "We got a picture": Jerry Hagstrom, "From Farm to Table," *Government Executive,* September 1, 1998. http:// www.govexec.com/features/0998/0998s4s2.htm

84 "the food stamp program": "The Safety Net: A History of Food Stamps Use and Policy," nytimes.com, February 11, 2010. http://www.nytimes.com/interactive/2010/ 02/11/us/FOODSTAMPS.html

85 "relentless": Interview, Paul Ryan.

85 more than 80 percent: CNN/ORC Poll, September 23– 25, 2011. http://www.pollingreport.com/social.htm; "Public Wants Change in Entitlements, Not Change in Benefits," Pew Research Center, July 7, 2011. http:// www.people-press.org/2011/07/07/section-5-views-of -social-security/

86 In contrast to: Social Security Administration, "Vote Tallies: 1935 Social Security Act." http://www.ssa.gov/ history/tally.html

86 "You cannot keep": Michael Lind, "Is Social Security a Ponzi Scheme?," nytimes.com, September 9, 2011.

http://www.nytimes.com/roomfordebate/2011/09/09/
is-social-security-a-ponzi-scheme

87 The number of taxpaying: http://www.socialsecurity
.gov/OACT/TR/2011/lr4b2.html

87 if nothing is done: http://www.ssa.gov/oact/TRSUM/
index.html

87 Nearly 55 million people: http://www.ssa.gov/press
office/basicfact.htm

88 Most who draw benefits: http://www.socialsecurity.gov/
policy/docs/quickfacts/stat_snapshot/index.html?qs

88 But nearly half: http://www.socialsecurity.gov/policy/
docs/statcomps/income_pop55/

88 "I feel like": Interview, Martha Soderberg.

90 "[A]fter 10 years": Letter from Leon Panetta to John
McCain, November 14, 2011. http://www.scribd.com/
doc/72831635/Panetta-McCain-Graham-Ltr

91 Skeptics were quick to note: Lawrence Korb, "The Real
Effects of Sequestration on Defense Spending," *Huffington Post,* November 17, 2011. http://www.huffingtonpost
.com/lawrence-korb/sequestration-defense-spending
_b_1100484.html

91 "We do not have": Bernard Brodie, *Strategy in the Missle
Age* (Santa Monica, Calif.: Rand Corp., 1959), 359–61.
Quoted in Todd Harrison, "$trategy in a Year of Fiscal
Uncertainty," Center for Strategic and Budgetary Assess-
ments, February 2012.

91 Aircraft carriers are expensive: Congressional Budget
Office, "Reducing the Deficit: Spending and Revenue
Options," March 2010, 90. http://www.cbo.gov/ftpdocs/
120xx/doc12085/03-10-ReducingTheDeficit.pdf

91 The navy calls them: Julian Barnes and Nathan Hodge,

"The New Arms Race: China Takes Aim at U.S. Naval Might," *Wall Street Journal,* January 4, 2012.

92 The new carriers: U.S. Navy Fact File: Aircraft Carriers. http://www.navy.mil/navydata/fact_display.asp?cid =4200&tid=200&ct=4

92 "The need to project": Remarks as delivered by Secretary of Defense Robert M. Gates, May 3, 2010. http:// www.defense.gov/speeches/speech.aspx?speechid=1460

93 Obama reportedly rejected: http://www.nytimes.com/ 2012/01/05/us/in-new-strategy-panetta-plans-even -smaller-army.html?_r=1

93 "The president feels": Interview, Leon Panetta.

93 In May 2010: Remarks as delivered by Secretary of Defense Robert Gates, Dwight D. Eisenhower Presidential Library, May 8, 2010. http://www.defense.gov/speeches/ speech.aspx?speechid=1467

94 as on the war in Iraq: http://www.fas.org/sgp/crs/nat sec/RL33110.pdf

94 Health care consumes: Lawrence Korb et al., *Restoring Tricare: Ensuring the Long Term Viability of the Military Health Care System* (Washington, D.C.: Center for American Progress, March 2010). http://www.americanprog ress.org/issues/2011/02/pdf/tricare.pdf

94 "meets with a furious": Remarks by Gates. http://www .defense.gov/speeches/speech.aspx?speechid=1467

94 "They've always been very strong": Interview, Leon Panetta.

95 Few outsiders appreciate: Congressional Budget Office, "Reducing the Deficit: Spending and Revenue Options," 80. http://www.cbo.gov/ftpdocs/120xx/doc12085/03- 10-ReducingTheDeficit.pdf

95 "Try to change": Belinda Luscombe, "Ten Questions for Alan Simpson," *Time,* August 8, 2011. http://www.time .com/time/magazine/article/0,9171,2084567,00.html

95 Obama's latest budget: Karen Parish, " 'Budget Request Preserves Troop Health Benefits,' Official Says," Department of Defense, February 14, 2012. http://www .defense.gov/news/newsarticle.aspx?id=67190

95 The health plan is so generous: http://www.cbo.gov/ sites/default/files/cbofiles/attachments/GrahamLetter 021712.pdf

95 "so cheap": Elisabeth Bumiller and Thom Shanker, "Gates Seeing to Contain Military Costs," *New York Times,* November 28, 2010.

96 "costing us $11 billion": Quoted in Amanda Palleschi, "Budget Request Includes TRICARE Cut, Military Retirement Details," *Government Executive,* February 13, 2012. http://www.govexec.com/defense/2012/02/budget -request-includes-tricare-cut-military-retirement-details/ 41193/print/

97 But 65 percent: Association for State Dam Safety Officials, "Dam Owners." http://damsafety.org/community/ owners/?p=e9a03866-a7b1–469a-83d8–27122057751a

97 "Many state dam safety programs": American Society of Civil Engineers, "America's Infrastructure Report Card." http://www.infrastructurereportcard.org/fact-sheet/ dams

98 South Dakota: Association of State Dam Safety Officials, "2010 Statistics on State Dam Safety Regulation," November 2011.http://www.damsafety.org/media/Documents/ STATE_INFO/State%20Performance%20Data/2010 _StateStats.pdf

98 A 1972 dam collapse: Association of State Dam Safety Officials, "Dam Failures, Dam Incidents." http://www .damsafety.org/media/Documents/STATE_INFO/State %20Performance%20Data/2010_StateStats.pdf

98 The Army Corps of Engineers: Army Corps of Engineers, "Dams by Hazard Potential." http://geo.usace .army.mil/pgis/f?p=397:5:3537652343623686::NO

98 And thus was born: Association of State Dam Safety Officials, "National Dam Safety Program Act of 2006." http://www.damsafety.org/media/Documents/Leg islative%20Handouts/2007-08/National%20Dam%20 Safety%20Program%20Act%2006.pdf

100 A 2011 Pew: Pew Research Center poll, June 15–19, 2011. http://www.people-press.org/files/legacy-question naires/June11%20space%20topline%20for%20release.pdf

100 Gallup poll: Gallup Inc., "Majority of Americans Say Space Program Costs Justified," July 17, 2009. http:// www.gallup.com/poll/121736/majority-americans-say -space-program-costs-justified.asp

100 "Space exploration": Barack Obama, "On Space Exploration in the 21st Century," April 15, 2010. http://www .nasa.gov/news/media/trans/obama_ksc_trans.html

101 "Every dollar": Charles Bolden, NASA budget briefing, February 13, 2012. Video is at http://www.c-span.org/ Events/NASA-Fiscal-Year-2013-Budget-Briefing/ 10737428275/

101 "The Mars program": Yudhijit Bhattacharjee, "Ed Weiler Says He Quit NASA Over Cuts to Mars Program," *Science Insider*, February 9, 2012. http://news.sciencemag.org/ scienceinsider/2012/02/ed-weiler-says-he-quit-nasa -over.html

102 "We could not": Charles Bolden, NASA budget briefing,

February 13, 2012. Video is at http://www.c-span.org/
Events/NASA-Fiscal-Year-2013-Budget-Briefing/
10737428275/

CHAPTER 4: WHERE THE MONEY COMES FROM

103 Joseph decreed: Genesis 47:26.

103 Large parts of the Rosetta Stone: Rosetta Stone transla-
tion by R. S. Simpson, Griffith Institute, Oxford University.
http://www.britishmuseum.org/explore/highlights/
article_index/r/the_rosetta_stone_translation.aspx

103 In the eighteenth century: W. R. Ward, "The Administration of the Window and Assessed Taxes, 1696–1798," *English
Historical Review* 68 (1952): 522–42. http://www.building
history.org/taxation.shtml

103 Peter the Great taxed: *Modern History Sourcebook: Peter the
Great and the Rise of Russia, 1682–1725,* Fordham University. http://www.fordham.edu/halsall/mod/petergreat.asp

103 In 1779, Britain: "A Tax to Beat Napoleon," HM Revenue
and Customs. http://www.hmrc.gov.uk/history/taxhis1
.htm

104 "After the income tax": Quoted in Daniel Gross, "A
Look Back at America's Time of Temperance," *News-
week,* June 6, 2010. http://www.thedailybeast.com/
newsweek/2010/06/01/a-look-back-at-america-s-time
-of-temperance.html

104 Initially, the income tax: Michael J. Graetz, *The U.S. In-
come Tax: What It Is, How It Got That Way, and Where
We Go from Here* (New York: W. W. Norton, 1997), 16.
Also see Bruce Bartlett, *The Benefit and the Burden: Tax
Reform–Why We Need It and What It Will Take* (New York:
Simon & Schuster, 2012), 249; and Tax Foundation, "Fed-

eral Individual Income Tax Rates History." http://www
.taxfoundation.org/files/fed_individual_rate_history
_nominal&adjusted-20110909.pdf

105 "Because of the need": Joel Slemrod and Jon Bakija, *Taxing Ourselves: A Citizen's Guide to the Great Debate over Tax Reform* (Cambridge, Mass.: MIT Press, 1996), 23.

105 In contrast: Corporation Income Tax Brackets and Rates, 1909–2002. http://www.irs.gov/pub/irs-soi/02corate.pdf

105 In the early 1950s: Bartlett, *Benefit and Burden,* 3–12.

106 That last factor: U.S. Treasury, "The President's Framework for Corporate Tax Reform," February 2012, 8. http://www.treasury.gov/resource-center/tax-policy/Documents/The-Presidents-Framework-for-Business-Tax-Reform-02-22-2012.pdf

107 For every $1: U.S. Census Bureau, "Quarterly Summary of State and Local Tax Revenue." http://www.census.gov/govs/qtax/

108 State and local governments: Tax Policy Center, "State and Local Tax Revenue as a Percentage of Personal Income, 1977–2009." http://www.taxpolicycenter.org/taxfacts/displayafact.cfm?Docid=511

108 At last count: Center for Responsive Politics, "Lobbying Database." http://www.opensecrets.org/lobby/

108 "Gore lost": Interview, Jon Talisman.

111 "It's very difficult": Interview, Grover Norquist.

111 Republicans who violate: "The Pledge: Grover Norquist's Hold on the GOP," *60 Minutes*, November 20, 2011. http://www.cbsnews.com/8301-18560_162-57327816/the-pledge-grover-norquists-hold-on-the-gop/

111 "I don't want to abolish": "Profile: Political Activist Grover Norquist," *Morning Edition,* NPR, May 25, 2001.

http://www.npr.org/templates/story/story.php?story
Id=1123439

111 He is funny: "Funniest Celebrity in Washington," September 30, 2009. http://www.youtube.com/watch?v
=WWs0wAuNPY8

112 When he successfully: Bernie Becker, "Vote to End
Ethanol Subsidies Revives Coburn-Norquist Tax Revenue Battle," *The Hill,* June 11, 2011. http://thehill.com/
blogs/on-the-money/domestic-taxes/165891-ethanol
-subsidies-revive-coburn-norquist-battle

112 "Which pledge is": *Meet the Press* transcript, April 24, 2011.
http://www.msnbc.msn.com/id/42703787/ns/meet
_the_press-transcripts/t/meet-press-transcript-april/;
also see Philip Klein, "A Brief History of the Coburn-
Norquist Tax Spat and Why It Matters," *Washington
Examiner,* April 25, 2011. http://washingtonexaminer
.com/blogs/beltway-confidential/2011/04/brief-his
tory-coburn-norquist-tax-spat-and-why-it-matters
#ixzz1l9502EUR

115 Their federal *income* taxes: http://www.cbo.gov/sites/
default/files/cbofiles/attachments/10-25-House
holdIncome.pdf

115 In 2011, about 40 percent: Tax Policy Center, "Distribution of Tax Units That Pay More in Payroll Taxes
Than Individual Income Taxes, by Cash Income Percentile, Current Law, 2011," June 17, 2011. http://www
.taxpolicycenter.org/numbers/displayatab.cfm?Docid
=3073&DocTypeID=2

116 separate estimates by the Tax Policy Center: Personal
communication, Tax Policy Center.

116 In December 2011: "Tax System Seen as Unfair, in Need

of Overhaul," Pew Research Center, December 20, 2011. http://www.people-press.org/2011/12/20/tax-system -seen-as-unfair-in-need-of-overhaul/; also see Gallup Poll, "Taxes," http://www.gallup.com/poll/1714/taxes.aspx

117 "Tax returns of the rich": Joseph J. Thorndike, "The Lessons of Mitt Romney's Tax Returns": CNN.com, January 26, 2012. http://money.cnn.com/2012/01/26/news/ economy/romney_tax_returns/index.htm

117 Romney's return revealed: Tax History Project, "Presidential Tax Returns." http://taxhistory.tax.org/www/web site.nsf/Web/PresidentialTaxReturns?OpenDocument

117 (taxed at a lower rate than wages): Tax Policy Center, "Average Effective Federal Tax Rates by Cash Income Percentiles, 2011 Baseline: Current Law," February 8, 2012. http://www.taxpolicycenter.org/numbers/display atab.cfm?Docid=3277

117 newspaper editors: "Question-and-Answer Session at the Annual Convention of the Associated Press Managing Editors Association, Orlando, Florida," November 17, 1973. http://www.presidency.ucsb.edu/ws/index.php?pid =4046&st=associated+press&st1=#axzz1td0m7mRJ

118 testimony by the Treasury secretary: Joseph W. Barr, "Statement of Hon. Joseph W. Barr, Secretary of the Treasury," in U.S. Congress, Joint Economic Committee, *Hearings on the 1969 Economic Report of the President, pt. 1, 91st Cong., 1st sess., January 17* (Washington, D.C.: Government Printing Office, 1969), 4–98. Also see Graetz, *U.S. Income Tax,* 113.

118 first AMT taxpayer: William D. Samons, "President Nixon's Troublesome Tax Returns," April 11, 2005. http:// www.taxhistory.org/thp/readings.nsf/cf7c9c870b600

b9585256df80075b9dd/f8723e3606cd79ec85256ff6006f
82c3?OpenDocument

119 Nixon's successor: Ibid.

119 "Those who have done well": "Remarks by the President on Economic Growth and Deficit Reduction," Rose Garden, September 19, 2011. http://www.whitehouse.gov/the-press-office/2011/09/19/remarks-president-economic-growth-and-deficit-reduction

119 "You know, there was": Mitt Romney at Iowa State Fair, transcript, August 11, 2011.

120 Here's where things stand today: Tax Policy Center, "Share of Taxes Paid by Filing Status and Demographics, Under Current Law, by Cash Income Percentile, 2011," February 2, 2012. http://www.taxpolicycenter.org/numbers/displayatab.cfm?Docid=3271

121 size of the slice: http://g-mond.parisschoolofeconomics.eu/topincomes

121 The snapshot for 2008: Internal Revenue Service, "The 400 Individual Income Tax Returns Reporting the Highest Adjusted Gross Incomes Each Year, 1992–2008." http://www.irs.gov/pub/irs-soi/08intop400.pdf

121 "The very rich": http://taxvox.taxpolicycenter.org/2011/05/12/the-very-rich-really-are-different/

121 Nearly 60 percent of their gross income: http://www.irs.gov/pub/irs-soi/08intop400.pdf

122 After food stamps: Internal Revenue Service, "Earned Income Tax Credit Statistics." http://www.eitc.irs.gov/central/eitcstats/

123 Weapons Supply Tax Credit: Edward Kleinbard, "The Congress Within the Congress: How Tax Expenditures Distort Our Budget and Our Political Processes," *Ohio*

Northern Law Review 6, no. 2 (2010): 1–30. http://web law.usc.edu/assets/docs/contribute/Kleinbard%20 ONU%20proofs%20Final.pdf

123 These "tax expenditures": Office of Management and Budget, *Fiscal Year 2013 Analytical Perspectives,* "Estimates of Total Income Tax Expenditures for Fiscal Years 2011–2017," Table 17–1. http://www.whitehouse.gov/sites/ default/files/omb/budget/fy2013/assets/spec.pdf

124 $2.3 trillion: Kleinbard, "The Congress Within the Congress," 26.

124 "It is just spending": Joint Select Committee on Deficit Reduction, *Hearing: Overview of Previous Debt Proposals,* November 1, 2011. http://www.c-span.org/Events/ Super-Committee-Looks-at-Past-Debt-Proposals/ 10737425140-1/

124 about 10 percent of the spending: Office of Management and Budget, *Fiscal Year 2013 Analytical Perspectives,* Table 17-1. http://www.whitehouse.gov/sites/default/ files/omb/budget/fy2013/assets/spec.pdf

124 If all the tax expenditures: Joint Committee on Taxation, memo, October 27, 2011. http://www.novoco.com/ hottopics/resource_files/jct-memo_tax-expenditure -repeal_102711.pdf

125 "All real estate": Congressional Research Service, "Tax Expenditures" (Washington, D.C.: Government Printing Office, 2007), 336. http://www.gpo.gov/fdsys/pkg/ CPRT-109SPRT31188/pdf/CPRT-109SPRT31188.pdf

125 The revenues lost: http://www.budget.senate.gov/demo cratic/index.cfm/files/serve?File_id=8a03a030-3ba8 -4835-a67b-9c4033c03ec4, p. 425.

125 "readily realizable market value": http://www.exeter1031 .com/history_section_1031.aspx

125 "If all exchanges": Quoted in Boris I. Bittker and Lawrence Lokken, *Federal Taxation of Income, Gifts and Trusts,
3d ed.* (Valhalla, N.Y: Warren, Gorham & Lamont, 2000),
Section 44.2.1, p. 564.

125 one can swap a dental office: Atlas 1031 Exchange LLC,
"The 1031 Exchange Blog: Medical, Dental and Vet-
erinary Practice 1031 Exchange." http://www.atlas1031
.com/blog/1031-exchange/bid/41380/Medical-Dental
-and-Veterinary-Practice-1031-Exchange

125 One can trade horses: Atlas 1031 Exchange LLC, "The
1031 Exchange Blog: Livestock Eligible for 1031 Exchange."
http://www.atlas1031.com/blog/1031-exchange/bid/
37086/Livestock-Eligible-for-1031-Exchange

126 "Livestock of different sexes": Internal Revenue Service,
"Like-Kind Exchanges–Real Estate Tax Tips," February 17, 2012. http://www.irs.gov/businesses/small/indus
tries/article/0,,id=98491,00.html

126 "any strategy for reducing": "HR. 1249: An Act to
Amend Title 35, United States Code, to Provide for Patent Reform," January 5, 2011, 44. http://www.uspto.gov/
aia_implementation/bills-112hr1249enr.pdf

127 "you can make": http://accruit.com/accruit-1031-single
-like-kind-exchanges/

127 Joe and Marilynn Croydon: Sam Smith, "Case Study:
1031 Exchanges and Vintage Motorcars," Accruit.com.
http://accruit.com/case-study-1031-exchanges-and
-vintage-motorcars/

CHAPTER 5: WHY THIS CAN'T GO ON FOREVER

129 "We're driving": Interview, Robert Reischauer.

131 "throwing $800 billion out the window": "Romney Cam-

paigns in New Hampshire," Money, CNN.com. http://
www.thebostonchannel.com/r/29327664/detail.html

132 CBO's latest price tag: Congressional Budget Office, *The
Budget and Economic Outlook: Fiscal Years 2012 to 2022*
(Washington, D.C.: Government Printing Office, Janu-
ary 2012), 9. http://www.cbo.gov/publication/42905

132 "No one would": David Weigel, "Douglas Holtz-Eakin:
'No One Would Argue That the Stimulus Has Done
Nothing,'" *Washington Independent,* August 9, 2009. http://
washingtonindependent.com/54312/douglas-holtz
-eakin-no-one-would-argue-that-the-stimulus-has-done
-nothing

133 "Suppose a patient": Christina D. Romer, "The Economy:
Where Are We and What Should We Do?," League of
Women Voters Annual Community Luncheon, Au-
gust 18, 2011. http://www.econ.berkeley.edu/~cromer/
The%20Economy%20Where%20Are%20We%20
and%20What%20Should%20We%20Do.pdf

133 Harvard's Larry Summers…Stanford's John Taylor:
Amanda E. McGowen, "Summers Debates Fiscal Policies," *Harvard Crimson,* February 29, 2012. http://www
.thecrimson.com/article/2012/2/29/Summers-Debates
-Fiscal-Policies/

134 A February 2012 survey: IGM Forum, "Economic
Stimulus," posted February 15, 2012. http://www.igm
chicago.org/igm-economic-experts-panel/poll-results
?SurveyID=SV_cw5O9LNJL1oz4Xi

134 "I'm a believer": Interview, Robert Reischauer.

134 In a February 2012 Pew poll: Pew Research Center for
the People & The Press, "February 2012 Political Survey,"
February 8–12, 2012. http://www.people-press.org/files/
legacy-questionnaires/2-23-12%20Topline.pdf

135 "Debt to the Penny": "Debt to the Penny–and Who Owns It." http://www.savingsbonds.gov/NP/NPGateway

135 "[T]ruth is": "Remarks by the President on the Budget," February 13, 2012. http://www.whitehouse.gov/the-press-office/2012/02/13/remarks-president-budget

136 Back in 1955: Office of Management and Budget, *Fiscal Year 2013 Analytical Perspectives,* "Federal Borrowing and Debt," 81.

137 Measured as a percentage: David Wessel, "What's Going on with Debt in the U.S.," wsj.com, January 23, 2012. http://blogs.wsj.com/economics/2012/01/23/whats-going-on-with-debt-in-u-s/

139 "If the Treasury": Simon Johnson and James Kwak, *White House Burning: The Founding Fathers, Our National Debt and Why It Matters to You* (New York: Pantheon Books, 2012), p. 123.

139 more than triple: Office of Management and Budget, *Fiscal Year 2013 Historical Tables,* Table 9–7. http://www.whitehouse.gov/omb/budget/Historicals

140 Budget Control Act: http://cbo.gov/publication/42214

143 "The good news": Interview, Doug Elmendorf.

143 "If a country": J. Bradford DeLong, "Budgeting and Macro Policy: A Primer," February 2, 2012, 12. http://delong.typepad.com/20120221-budgeting-and-macro-policy-a-primer.pdf

144 "transcendent threat": Peter G. Peterson remarks, May 15, 2012. http://www.pgpf.org/Issues/Fiscal-Outlook/2012/05/051512-FS-Pete-Remarks.aspx

145 Drawn to economics: Interview with Paul Krugman, nobelprize.org, December 6, 2008. http://www.nobelprize.org/mediaplayer/index.php?id=1049

145 "How many bills": Ryan Lizza, "Letter from Washing-

ton: The Gatekeeper," *New Yorker,* March 2, 2009. http://
www.newyorker.com/reporting/2009/03/02/090302fa
_fact_lizza?currentPage=all

145 "The question is": Jane Hamsher, "Krugman Responds
to Rahm Emanuel," Firedoglake.com, February 22, 2009.
http://firedoglake.com/2009/02/22/krugman-responds
-to-rahm-emanuel/

146 "Premature deficit reduction": Paul Krugman, "Notes
on Deleveraging," *The Conscience of a Liberal,* January 22,
2012. http://krugman.blogs.nytimes.com/2012/01/22/
notes-on-deleveraging/

147 "You shouldn't put": Interview, Paul Ryan.

148 "a strange combination": Paul Krugman, "Paul Ryan's
Multiple Unicorns," *The Conscience of a Liberal,* April 6,
2001. http://krugman.blogs.nytimes.com/2011/04/06/
PAUL-RYANS-MULTIPLE-UNICORNS/

148 "I believe the way": Interview, Paul Ryan.

148 "My daughter jokes": Peter G. Peterson, *The Education of
an American Dreamer* (New York: Hachette Book Group,
2009), p 347.

149 "the godfather": Alan Feuer, "Peter G. Peterson's Last Anti-
Debt Campaign," *New York Times,* April 10, 2011, MB1.
http://www.nytimes.com/2011/04/10/nyregion/10
peterson.html?pagewanted=all

150 "too much of an all-or-nothing": Leonard Silk, "Political Costs of Reagan Cuts," *New York Times,* March 20,
1981.

150 "a growing systemic inability": Peter G. Peterson, "Spending Limits," *New York Times,* July 23, 1981.

150 "playing golf": Interview, Peter Peterson.

150 "engage the American people": Peter G. Peterson Foun-

dation, "Q&A with Pete Peterson," October 7, 2011. http://www.pgpf.org/Issues/Fiscal-Outlook/2011/06/ QA-with-Peter-Peterson.aspx?p=1

151 "On our current course": "A Letter from Peter G. Peterson to the Super Committee," November 2, 2011. http://www.pgpf.org/Issues/Fiscal-Outlook/2011/11/110211 _Letter-to-Super-Committee.aspx

152 "Unlike some of my Wall Street": Peter G. Peterson, "Facing Up," *The Atlantic,* October 1993. http://www .theatlantic.com/past/politics/budget/facingf.htm

152 "objective economic advice": Robert Stanley Herren, "Council of Economic Advisers," EH.net, Encyclopedia. http://eh.net/encyclopedia/article/herren.cea

152 "The first recession": Christina D. Romer, "Not My Father's Recession: The Extraordinary Challenges and Policy Responses of the First Twenty Months of the Obama Administration," National Press Club, September 1, 2010. http://www.whitehouse.gov/sites/default/ files/microsites/100901-National-Press-Club.pdf

153 "The evidence is stronger": Christina D. Romer, "What Do We Know About the Effects of Fiscal Policy? Separating Evidence from Ideology," Hamilton College, November 7, 2011. http://www.econ.berkeley.edu/~cromer/ Written%20Version%20of%20Effects%20of%20Fiscal %20Policy.pdf

154 "We don't have to": Christina Romer, "The Economy: Where Are We and What Should We Do," League of Women Voters Annual Community Luncheon, August 18, 2011. http://elsa.berkeley.edu/~cromer/The%20 Economy%20Where%20Are%20We%20and%20What %20Should%20We%20Do.pdf

154 "a two-handed plan": Ben Bernanke at House Committee on Financial Services, February 29, 2012.

155 "a geek with guts": Sheryl Gay Stolberg, "Capital Holds
Breath as He Crunches Numbers," *New York Times,* November 17, 2009.

155 "A quiet man": Ibid.

156 "You want to be sure": Interview, Doug Elmendorf.

157 "Why wouldn't one conclude": "The Budget and Economic Outlook: Fiscal Years 2012–2022," Hearing of the
Senate Budget Committee, February 2, 2012.

157 "I don't want to speak": Ibid.

157 "We cannot go back": Interview, Doug Elmendorf.

158 "The country faces": David Wessel, "The Federal Deficit Mess in a Single Sentence," wsj.com, November 11,
2009. http://blogs.wsj.com/washwire/2009/11/11/the
-federal-deficit-mess-in-a-single-sentence/

159 "The country": Interview, Douglas Elmendorf.

162 "I used to tell the students": Interview, Leon Panetta.

BIBLIOGRAPHY

In addition to the publications and websites of the White House Office of Management and Budget, the Congressional Budget Office, the Tax Policy Center, the Committee for a Responsible Federal Budget, the Bipartisan Policy Center, the Center on Budget and Policy Priorities, and the Peter G. Peterson Foundation, the following books provided valuable context and explanation.

Bartlett, Bruce. *The Benefit and the Burden: Tax Reform—Why We Need It and What It Will Take.* New York: Simon & Schuster, 2012.

Dame, Philip R., and Bernard H. Martin. *The Evolution of OMB.* Privately published, Washington, D.C., 2009.

Darman, Richard. *Who's in Control? Polar Politics and the Sensible Center.* New York: Simon & Schuster, 1996.

Graetz, Michael J. *The U.S. Income Tax: What It Is, How It Got That Way, and Where We Go from Here.* New York: W. W. Norton, 1997.

Hager, George, and Eric Pianin. *Mirage: Why Neither Demo-*

crats nor Republicans Can Balance the Budget, End the Deficit, and Satisfy the Public. New York: Times Books, 1997.

Johnson, Simon, and James Kwak. *White House Burning: The Founding Fathers, Our National Debt, and Why It Matters to You.* New York: Pantheon Books, 2012.

Joyce, Philip G. *The Congressional Budget Office: Honest Numbers, Power, and Policymaking.* Washington, D.C.: Georgetown University Press, 2011.

Panetta, Leon, and Peter Gall. *Bring Us Together: The Nixon Team and the Civil Rights Retreat.* New York: J. B. Lippincott Co., 1971.

Peterson, Peter G. *The Education of an American Dreamer: How a Son of Greek Immigrants Learned His Way from a Nebraska Diner to Washington, Wall Street, and Beyond.* New York: Hachette Book Group, 2009.

Scheiber, Noam. *The Escape Artists: How Obama's Team Fumbled the Recovery.* New York: Simon & Schuster, 2012.

Schick, Allen. *The Federal Budget: Politics, Policy, Process.* Washington, D.C.: The Brookings Institution, 2000.

Slemrod, Joel, and Jon Bakija. *Taxing Ourselves: A Citizen's Guide to the Great Debate over Tax Reform.* Cambridge, Mass.: MIT Press, 1996.

Stein, Herbert. *The Fiscal Revolution in America: Policy in Pursuit of Reality.* Washington, D.C.: American Enterprise Institute Press, 1996.

Stockman, David A. *The Triumph of Politics: Why the Reagan Revolution Failed.* New York: Harper & Row, 1986.

ACKNOWLEDGMENTS

In a sense, I have been working on this book for the twenty-five years I've been an economics reporter in Washington, a pursuit that depends in part on the willingness of budget experts in and out of government to field reporters' questions and offer instruction. Among those on whom I have relied over the years and to whom I turned in researching this book were Barry Anderson, Ken Baer, Steve Bell, Stanley Collander, Robert Greenstein, Bill Hoagland, James Horney, Robert Reischauer, Gene Sperling, Douglas Holtz-Eakin, Douglas Elmendorf, Donald Marron, Todd Harrison, Allen Schick, Eugene Steuerle, Conor Sweeney, Susan Tanaka, Eric Toder—and several others who prefer not to be named. Among the reporters on the budget beat whose thorough work I consulted for perspective and detail were Naftali Bendavid, Jackie Calmes, Nathan Hodge, Janet Hook, Ryan Lizza, Lori Montgomery, Dan Morgan, Damian Paletta, Eric Pianin, David Rogers, and Noam Scheiber.

ACKNOWLEDGMENTS

My agent, Raphael Sagalyn, sparked this book, and was a constant and valued counselor from start to finish. Howard and Nathan Means were extremely efficient and perceptive editors, helpful on matters large and small. Roger Scholl at Crown Books was an enthusiastic supporter, offering his advice at key moments. Able copy editor Maureen Clark fixed broken sentences and caught careless errors. Veteran budget reporters Jackie Calmes of the *New York Times* and Janet Hook of the *Wall Street Journal* generously read the manuscript and offered suggestions. Nelson Hsu turned my ideas into clear and attractive charts. Benjamin Grazda, Spencer Wright, and Lois Parshley were agile and conscientious research assistants. The Woodrow Wilson Center for International Scholars provided a quiet place to work and resourceful librarians. The editors of the *Wall Street Journal,* which remains the best place to practice daily journalism, granted me a leave without which this book would not have been possible. Any mistakes are my responsibility alone.

Book-writing is hard on spouses. This book is no exception. My wife, Naomi, put up with my absence, crabbiness, and sleepless nights without complaint, and I love her for that and for many other reasons.

INDEX

ABOUT THE AUTHOR

David Wessel is economics editor for the *Wall Street Journal* and writes the Capital column (wsj.com/capital), a weekly look at the economy and forces shaping living standards around the world. He appears frequently on National Public Radio's *Morning Edition* and on WETA's *Washington Week*. He tweets actively at www.twitter.com/davidmwessel.

Previously, Wessel was deputy bureau chief of the *Wall Street Journal*'s Washington bureau. He joined the *Wall Street Journal* in 1984 in Boston, and moved to Washington in 1987. In 1999 and 2000 he served as the newspaper's Berlin bureau chief. He previously worked for the *Boston Globe,* as well as the *Hartford Courant* and the *Middleton Press* in Connecticut.

Wessel has shared two Pulitzer Prizes, one for *Boston Globe* stories in 1983 on the persistence of racism in Boston and the other for stories in the *Wall Street Journal* in 2002 on corporate wrongdoing.

His book *In Fed We Trust: Ben Bernanke's War on the Great Panic* was selected by the *New York Times* as one of the 100 Notable Books of 2008. He is also the coauthor, with *Wall Street Journal* reporter Bob Davis, of *Prosperity,* a 1998 book on the American middle class.

A product of the New Haven, Connecticut, public schools and a 1975 graduate of Haverford College, he was a Knight Bagehot fellow in business and economic journalism at Columbia University in 1980–1981. Wessel and his wife, Naomi Karp, have two children, Julia and Ben. His website is www.davidwessel.net.

A penetrating, inside look at how the Fed
spearheaded the biggest government intervention
in more than half a century to prevent the world's
financial engine from grinding to a halt

A *NEW YORK TIMES*
NOTABLE BOOK

"An engrossing account."
—*FORTUNE*

"A gripping blow-
by-blow account....
A cracking story, the
best chronicle so far."
—*THE ECONOMIST*

"Essential, lucid ...
riveting."
—*NEW YORK TIMES*

For more than twenty years, David Wessel has been the *Wall Street Journal*'s
insider at the Federal Reserve. With continual access to its chairmen, gov-
ernors, policy makers, and staffers, Wessel has an insider's view of the biggest ongoing story of our time.

A perceptive look at a historic episode in American and global economic
history, *In Fed We Trust* illuminates this drama in terms you don't need to
be a Wall Street insider to grasp.

AVAILABLE WHEREVER
BOOKS ARE SOLD

Printed in the United States
by Baker & Taylor Publisher Services